LEADERSHIP

The Multiplier Effect

••••••

ANDY COPE, MIKE MARTIN &
JONATHAN PEACH

First published in Great Britain in 2018 by John Murray Learning.
An Hachette UK company.

This edition published in 2019 by John Murray Learning.

British Library Cataloguing in Publication Data: a catalogue record for this title is available from the British Library.

Library of Congress Catalog Card Number: on file.

Hardback ISBN 978 1 473 67945 0

Paperback ISBN 978 1 473 69569 6

eISBN 978 1 473 67946 7

1

Typeset by Integra Software Services Pvt. Ltd.

Printed and bound in Great Britain by Clays Ltd, Elcograf S.p.A.

John Murray Learning policy is to use papers that are natural, renewable and recyclable products and made from wood grown in sustainable forests. The logging and manufacturing processes are expected to conform to the environmental regulations of the country of origin.

Carmelite House
50 Victoria Embankment
London EC4Y 0DZ

www.hodder.co.uk

LEADERSHIP

The Multiplier Effect

For Peter Anderton. A man whose principles are so strong that he stepped away from this book on the grounds that it contains a couple of naughty words.

#Respect.
Top banana.

CONTENTS

●●●●●●

THE BIT THAT NOBODY READS (BUT YOU REALLY SHOULD)

Thank you and welcome. Isn't it amazing how very patiently a book will wait to be read?

Three quick asides before the off ...

First, we've twigged that books sell well when they tell you what you want to hear. Our editor says it's usual to butter you up, so here goes – leadership is complex. It's a tough gig, hence you get paid more. The responsibilities are heavy. Leaders are the new superheroes – you have to be flexible, sharp, empathetic and super intelligent. Much cleverer than your employees, for sure.

In the modern world, that last bit is most probably untrue. It's important for you to know that we're going to continue to tell you the truth, and nothing but, throughout. Even if it's not what you want to hear.

Second, something you already know – your influence as a leader is massive. It has a huge multiplier effect. A leader in a positive mood cascades far and wide. If the whole organization is feeling good, everyone is optimistic, making good decisions and being creative then, *wham*, that's a superbly productive day.

As Bruce Forsyth used to say, '*and that's all there is to it*'. If only it was that easy?

While physics has immutable laws, 'people' are a law unto themselves. So, yes, on a good day you will have a multiplier effect but the reverse is also true – bad leaders can also have a subtraction and division effect!

By the time we're old enough to enter the workplace we have developed into emotional, walking, talking, lumbering habit machines. We've got a sense of who we are and what we're good and bad at. Most functioning adults also have a canny knack of being able to imagine how others perceive us, which gives rise to a whole load of issues around self-consciousness and embarrassment. In short, we all end up with an identity. If you want to change 'who you are' in the truest personal development sense of 'leaning into being your best self' then it's worth analogizing that life's not a nippy speedboat zipping about on a millpond sea – you're carrying a lifetime of emotional and psychological cargo being hauled across the vast oceans of your unconscious. We want to provide you with some quick wins, but a lot of personal change takes time, courage and practice so please expect a fair bit of sloshing around.

And third, something you didn't know – Apple Inc. will go rotten. Yes, it's a ridiculous statement. In every leadership and/or business book written in the last ten years Apple has been held up as a model of how to do things. Steve Jobs is some sort of a demi-god, worshipped as a creative visionary who invented simplicity. Apple, the most profitable company in the history of profitable companies, the organization that has an income greater than the entire 1977 US stock market, the company who is bigger than the GDP of Slovakia... and here we are, leadership small-fry, suggesting that Apple's going to go belly up. What's more, we're even daring to suggest that it'll happen a lot sooner than you think.

How do we know? Because nothing is permanent. Change has quickened to the point that business cycles are shortening, global competition is like a pack of rabid dogs and, sooner or later, Apple will get bitten. Some other company will emerge as the 'new Apple', headed by the 'new Steve Jobs' and historians will look back at these two paragraphs and coo at our foresight.

So, as the world quickens, what are we supposed to do? I think the trick is to enjoy the hurly-burly as life hurtles by in a blur. Be proud in the knowledge that historians will look back at us and go *Wow! They really were in the eye of the storm. They coped with the advent of the internet, all you can eat data, e-commerce and Brexit. They grappled with social media, global warming, oh, and the fall of Apple.*

Our point, before the off, is that you are leading in extraordinary times. So a top tip that also happens to be a recurring theme of this book: remember that in 40 years' time, you will reflect back on now as 'the good old days' so take time to enjoy today, today.

The challenge:

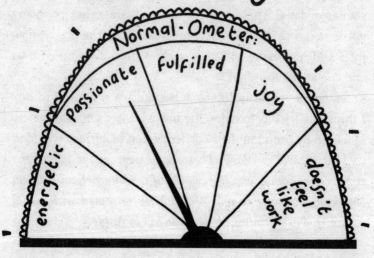

Chapter 1

JUST *ONE THING* TO REMEMBER

• • • • • •

It's all hectic days and Russian dolls to start with, plus a reminder to *not forget your towel*. We explain why working 24/7 isn't such a bad idea and ditch some tired leadership notions into Orwell's Room 101.

Chapter 1 challenges you to shine as well as rise, while also explaining why a third of roller-coaster riders are ill before they start. You'll notice our penchant for fairytale endings, albeit with dwarves and frogs along the way. There are also bulls and sheep (excellent ones).

Yes dear reader, Chapter 1 sets the standard. You'll notice that absolutely everything you'd expect from a 'normal' leadership book is completely absent, a point that we hope you think is wonderful.

Now what was that one thing I needed to remember again...?

Andy Cope, Mike Martin & Jonathan Peach

The Hitchhiker's Guide to Leadership

······

'WE HAVE THE MOST WONDERFUL JOB IN THE WORLD. WE FIND PEOPLE IN VARIOUS STAGES OF SLEEP. AND THEN WE GET TO TAP THEM ON THE SHOULDER AND BE WITH THEM AS THEY WAKE UP TO THE MAGNIFICENCE OF LIFE.'

······

Sydney Banks

You might be a big reader (someone who reads a lot of books, not a fat one). Or, you might not be.

It doesn't matter. All that matters is that you read this one. We've gone to the trouble of designing it so it's very readable. It's got everything that a 'normal' book has – words, pictures, paragraphs, punctuation – everything that is, except a story.

A book without a story? Waddayamean, it's not got a story? How can a book not have a story?

Just to confuse you, it has, and it hasn't. It's not got a story as in *boy wins ticket to chocolate factory and fat kid gets stuck in a tube along the way*. Its story is YOU. Yes, YOU are the central character. The only character really. YOU are not only in it, but you are the glue that holds the story together.

Which is where things really hot up. We want your leadership story to be one of action, excitement, adventure and fun. We want it to be one of those magical fairy tales where you inspire your team, give epic customer service and live happily ever after. You might have to kiss a few yukky frogs or live with seven dwarves somewhere along the way, but that's part of the adventure.

Too many folk have a rather dull leadership story. They 'live' a rather unspectacular corporate life; limping from one day to the next. Kissing frogs once in a while is just about bearable, but snogging them every day? Not good.

We wrote 'live' in inverted commas because it's important to know the difference between 'being alive' and 'living'. You see, technically speaking, you can be alive (showing all the classic signs: breathing, moving, eating toast, etc.) without really living. We figure that if you're going to the trouble of being alive, you should upgrade to '*properly* living'. It's more than having a pulse. It's about energy, passion, motivation, effort, colour, excitement, frogs and dwarves.

Make that pulse race a bit.

So, congrats, you're alive. But are you really living?

In *The Hitchhiker's Guide to the Galaxy*,[1] a person who can stay in control of virtually any situation is somebody who is said to know where his or her towel is; Douglas Adams's genius logic being that a towel has immense psychological value. If you pick up an intergalactic hitchhiker who has their towel with them, you will automatically assume that they are also in possession of a toothbrush, flannel, soap, sandwiches, flask, compass, map, alien repellent, cagoule, space suit, etc. It gives you faith. Burrowing deeper into the assumption, anyone who can hitch the length and breadth of the galaxy, rough it, slum it, struggle against terrible odds, win through, and still knows where their towel is, is clearly someone to be reckoned with.

Think of this book as your intergalactic towel. Yes, the modern world is bonkers but this book will give you a certain presence which will make you someone to be reckoned with.

The Most Excellent Sheep

So let's start with someone who's lost their towel.

Here's a classic family story, witnessed up and down the land. If you've got kids, you'll be familiar with it. If you've not, you'll still be familiar with it. Picture the typical hectic Monday morning scene as the family goes through their 'getting ready for school and work' routine. And then, while mum is simultaneously making packed lunches and ironing shirts, the daughter pushes away her untouched and now silent Rice Krispies and utters the dreaded, '*I'm not feeling very well*'.

The daughter makes sure to put on her feeble voice as part of the convincer strategy. Of course, mum's wise to this. It's a game. Her daughter has previous. This mysterious illness often crops up on a Monday when her daughter just happens to have a very busy timetable. And there's something else to add into the mix. Mum's day is already full. She has an important and unmoveable appointment so staying back to look after her 'poorly' daughter is not going to be possible. So mum does what all half-decent mums do: she feigns concern and puts her hand on her daughter's forehead and attempts the classic fob-off. *'You're a teensy bit warm but I think the walk will do you good.'*

'I'm really poorly, honest mum,' she wails through sad eyes. *'I really don't want to go in today.'*

Mum sighs. *'We've been through this before, Angie. You can't just skive off.'*

The girl whines some more. *'But whhhhhyyy?'* she wails, burying her face in her iPad.

'Because you're the manager!'

Now, if you're in a position of authority at work, you will have had mornings like this. As a leader, you have contracted a horrible disease called 'responsibility'. Chances are that someone higher up the food chain is saying, *'Here are some responsibilities. We're not taking any of the old ones away, mind. And here's a few whopping targets and slightly less budget than you had last year. And here's your team. Go make some brilliant things happen.'* Gulp! And, at a lucky guess, you've reached a tipping point where you can't work any harder? And, let me guess, if I ask you to work 'smarter' you're going to rip my throat out?

You've streamlined everything in an attempt to be super-efficient. You have an email system, with lots of little yellow folders. And, if you're super-duper efficient, you will have developed the 'Russian Doll' system whereby some of your little yellow folders have little yellow folders in them? Your fool-proof method of organizing your emails has created a bit more time, but that extra time will not be spent luxuriating on the team strategy or coaching your best people – it will simply be filled with even more emails. So, here's a clue upfront. Sending emails is not your purpose (more of that later).

The likely result of this tumultuous workload is that you're exhausted. When your alarm rudely awakens you at 6am on a winter's morning you don't leap out of bed with a *'Woohoo! Another Monday. Another opportunity to inspire my team and provide world class customer service.'* Nope. Your lustre is lacking and you need an energy transfusion. Most people groggily hit the snooze button in a desperate attempt to grab another nine minutes and 59 seconds of slumber before they drag their carcass out of bed.

Your commute is unlikely to be one of peace and joy. You might be one of the train commuters. Overground is bad enough, but underground? Crammed with people, nose to armpit, with no fresh air, shooting through a metal tube at 40mph. If you were pigs, sheep or cows the animal rights' folk would have it banned. Inhumane treatment. But because you're going to work it's somehow okay?

Of course, it's not just work. 'Busyness' applies to life. We get irritated by slowness. Your microwave meal's instructions tell you to cook it for two mins, then remove, stir and let it do another two – and you get angry that your evening meal is going to take so bloody long. Are you a digital lemming who gets home from work and immediately logs onto their emails?

Let's not pull any punches. We'd dare to suggest that life's not just exhausting, it's actually unfair, with managerial life doubly cruel. We tend to agree with Dennis Wholey who once said: *'Expecting the world to treat you fairly because you are good is like expecting the bull not to charge because you are a vegetarian.'*

Top Tip

To cut your 'to-do' list in half, simply get your to-do list and cut it in half. (Get a grown-up to help with the scissors.) #ArdaghTips

Life can feel like a Mexican stand-off: you versus life – who's gonna blink first?

While we're in 'no punches pulled' mode, we'll tell you straight, *it ain't gonna be life.* Life's just going to keep coming at you. The trick is to mould yourself around it, to craft a life worth living. One of abundance, energy and optimism that might not quite reach fairy tale proportions but it does end in a happily ever after.

But how? When the modern world is loaded against us. How do we flourish, against the odds?

The short answer is that it's perfectly possible, but it requires a re-think of our thinking, a re-calibration of our attitudes and a step up in behaviours. Here's a quirky sentence that sums up the rest of the book: *if more of the same isn't the answer, then maybe we need to re-focus to less of something different.*

It's comforting to appreciate that human beings have always been fighting against the odds. Our ancestors faced the very real physical dangers of hunting for their supper. A bad day at work meant a starving tribe, or worse. Instead of bringing home the bacon, you *were* the bacon!

It wasn't that long ago that industry was invented. Dickensian factories, child labour, belching fumes, insanitary hell holes. Nowadays it's a rare sight to see children up chimneys or employees devoid of personal protective equipment, toiling in intolerable conditions. Instead of slogging it out down the pit at the coalface we've become prisoners in a digital chain gang, hacking away at the typeface.

The miners might have had it tough but at least they didn't have to attend back-to-back meetings before commuting home and logging onto their emails. In the blink of an historical eye, physical danger has been replaced by mental danger. We see it every day. Schools, hospitals, businesses – their budgets are stretched to breaking point. It's a huge invisible irony – they can't afford more staff because they're already employing dozens of agency and temporary workers to cover for the ones who are off with stress, burnout or mental illness.

While the toxic fumes might now be filtered out, our physical safety has been secured at the cost of our mental safety with 'busyness' and 'infomania' hovering above us like some spectral death-figure.

Your author tag team are all very much of the real world. Indeed, this reality is our starting point. We're equipping you with knowledge and skills for the world as it is, not the world from ten years ago. We're sending you out there to swash-buckle against the odds. We're not promising it's going to be easy, but we can hand-on-heartedly tell you it'll be worth it.

> Chill ...
>
> *My new boss told me he expects me to be on call 24/7 but I don't really mind as July 24th is ages away.*

Chances are, staff numbers have been butchered to the point that there is no slack in the system and everyone is at full throttle. So here's what we do – human beings look around at what everyone else is doing ... *and copy*. As William Deresiewicz rightly points out, we become the world's most excellent sheep.[2]

If insanity means you keep doing what you've always done while expecting a different result, then current organizational behaviours are the preserve of Mad Hatters. Take a furtive glance at your work colleagues and fellow commuters. What do you want to be? Fuelled by caffeine and sugar, popping happy pills, on your third marriage and fourth heart murmur? A most excellent sheep, or safely in possession of your towel?

We're going to come at things from a different angle. We think people are silently begging to be led but the problem is that things can get a little complex. Most books are 'additive', giving you theories, principles and concepts to remember and apply. In the past you might, for example, have had to learn and remember seven habits, five levels, ten commandments, eight laws, twelve principles or whether you're an ISTJ or an ENFP.

As a big fat 'thank you' for buying our book, we will treat you to some 'subtractive psychology'. Less is more. Let's help take some shit off you. We want to give you *less* to think about, *less* to do and take things *off* your mind. Possibly, heaven forbid, take yourself and life *less* seriously?

Ask yourself, all those years of 'doing more' – those seven habits, five levels, ten commandments, eight laws and twelve principles. Has it worked? When you went on a workshop and discovered you were an EFNJ, did it change your life? Or you could have spent a day with a very expensive consultant learning whether you were a horse, lion or monkey. Or a colour, perhaps?

Nice one. Has it helped? Have you rumbled the secret and become God's gift to leadership?

Or is life just full-on exhausting?

Baa-aa.

Leadership is an education. And the best leaders think of themselves as the students, not the teachers.

All your worldly problems may seem complicated. But what if they're not? What if they can all be solved with some common sense, wrapped in fluffy insight, bounded by some soft padding of simplicity.

Wouldn't that make a nice change?

Yes, in a radical detour from 'normal' leadership books, we're going to give you less to bleat about and less to do. *Oh joy!* We're going to be consigning a whole raft of tired olde worlde leadership ideas to George Orwell's fabled Room 101, a darkened place where your worst leadership nightmares can be laid to rest. Our view is that the brave '*newe worlde*' requires a rethink and an injection of mojo-enhancement.

So here's our first offering for Room 101 of leadership bunkum: we give you the overblown notion that, as a leader, your job is to inspire people. Carrying that particular yoke of responsibility is so pressurized and exhausting – it's no wonder your shoulders are sagging.

We'd rather you change your focus. We believe David Taylor and Steve Radcliffe are both correct in suggesting that the leader's job is not to inspire people, but to *be inspired*.[3] This is much more than a clever play on words and we want to prove what you already know – once you release the pressure valve of having to inspire your people, it allows you to work on inspiring the only person you can really take charge of – yourself. And, guess what, in a serendipitous alignment of the planets, you will accidentally inspire your team.

Zombie-Land

The science of positive psychology has a habit of proving what we already intuitively know. For example:

- Happy people get sick less often (and when they do get ill, they recover faster).
- Happy people have more energy.
- Happy people are more optimistic.
- Happy people are more motivated.
- Happy people work better with others.

- Happy people are more creative.
- Happy people learn faster.
- Happy people make better decisions.

Now simply turn the positive statements above to negatives, and you get the workforce from hell! Is it really in anyone's interest to have a negative, uncreative, sickness-prone, pessimistic, lack-lustre, sclerotic, depressed workforce?

We work in organizations every day and have noticed an awful lot of mismatch between what is said and what is real. The way we run businesses is being stretched beyond breaking point. People at the bottom of the hierarchy have a job rather than a career and are clocking on for a shift of toil. It's often dread and drudgery rather than joy and passion. But here's a dirty little secret: it's exactly the same at the top, except the hourly rate is a bit higher. Behind the façade there is a lot of gnashing of teeth and quiet suffering. Frantic activity, yes, but this is often papering over the cracks of discontent, burnout and emptiness. Restructures, competitive pressures, corporate politics, negativity, long hours, targets ... it's all a big game.

Smonday ...

The moment when Sunday stops feeling like a Sunday and the anxiety of Monday kicks in.

The result of these frustrating and joyless workplaces is that staff spend too many working hours dreaming about their next holiday or counting down to retirement. You can take your pick of the studies. A survey of 32,000 employees found that 43 per cent were detached or actively disengaged, with 22 per cent feeling unsupported.[4] In short, they'd really rather not be there. Another suggests that a paltry 19 per cent of employees are actually engaged in their work.[5]

Working the numbers the other way, David Bolchover estimates that 19 per cent of employees are actively *disengaged* at work, 'the living dead', with a significant chunk (a further 62 per cent) reporting being neither engaged or disengaged and spend their time at work:

- Taking drugs (one in three workers).
- Having sex (one in five).
- Accessing internet porn (70 per cent of these hits occur during working hours).
- Visiting theme parks (one in three midweek visitors is 'off sick').
- 'Constantly' surfing the internet (one in five).[6]

Yes I know it sounds tempting and you're thinking you'd rather like one of those sex/drugs/porn/themepark type jobs? But actually, when push comes to shove, you wouldn't.

These people are your clock watchers who are likely to have a *'bad case of the Mondays'*. The problem with the 'living dead' is that they are not just disengaged at work, they are also likely to badmouth your organization to family and friends.

······

'NOTHING SAYS 'PUNCH ME' LIKE A CHEERY FACE BEFORE 9.00 AM.'

······

Philip Ardagh

In this brave new world, the 'undead' add a subtle nuance to the art of leadership. The workplace has changed. Rapidly and a lot. Few managers are required to negotiate with unions any longer, but nearly all of them confront a much trickier challenge; of dealing with employees who are regularly absent, unmotivated or suffering from persistent, low-level mental health problems. Back in the day, management was so much simpler. Loud-mouthed managers (invariably men) issued a strong verbal rebuke to the 'slackers'. Nowadays that's taboo, tantamount to bullying and six months off with stress. Resistance to work no longer manifests itself in an organized voice or outright refusal, but in insipid attitudes, apathy and chronic health problems. Some estimates suggest that over a third of European and American adults are suffering from some form of mental health problem.[7]

If you're not off with stress you're struggling to fill the extra workload created by those who are. The relentless pursuit of 'results' has created a murky grey area between simple workplace apathy and clinical disorder. Exhaustion is the new black.

Nigel Marsh's words might sound harsh, but he's not a million miles away with: 'Thousands of people are living lives of screaming desperation where they work long hours at jobs they hate to enable them to buy things they don't need to impress people they don't like.'[8]

David Hare describes it as painting over the rust.[9] Often 'well-being' strategies are not strategies at all – having a dress down Friday is the thinnest coating of gloss on the rustiest girder of discontentment and exhaustion.

······

'PUT THE KEY OF DESPAIR INTO THE LOCK OF APATHY. TURN THE KNOB OF MEDIOCRITY AND OPEN THE GATES OF DESPONDENCY – WELCOME TO THE DAY IN THE AVERAGE OFFICE.'

······

David Brent

Before we delve into solutions, it's apposite to pose some very big questions. Could it be that our current worldview limits the way we think about organizations? We're at pains to point out that the world has moved on very swiftly. Could it be that our thinking has lagged? Indeed, if we were to take today's business organizations and start again, would we design them the same? Would we manage them the same?

It's possible that current organizational learning has gained proverbial stretch marks. The organization, and its workforce, has been pushed beyond what it can comfortably cope with.

······

'THE GREATEST DANGER IN TIMES OF TURBULENCE IS NOT THE TURBULENCE – IT IS TO ACT WITH YESTERDAY'S LOGIC.'

······

Peter Drucker

So, back to some more knee-shakingly huge questions. Can we create organizations that are free of the pathologies that show up in life? *Imagine.* Free of bureaucracy, burnout, resentment and apathy? Is it possible to create a new kind of organization that makes work productive, fulfilling, meaningful and purposeful; where staff play to their strengths and are challenged in just the way they like to be challenged? In short, is it possible to create a workplace where work doesn't feel like work?

Our short answer is 'yes'. In fact, most organizations already achieve it – *sometimes!* We have all experienced days of heady joy where, whisper it quietly, but it was so fabulous that you'd have done it for free. Mountains of work got done, everyone was smiling and you felt invigorated rather than exhausted.

But then we go back to 'normal', that sense of surviving until the weekend, or your next holiday, accidentally wishing your life away. The challenge is to reset 'normal', away from 'mundane and lacklustre' towards 'vigorous and passionate'.

And we come full circle to the difference between 'being alive' and 'living'. One involves a pulse. The other involves a whole mind/body immersive experience in this adventure we call 'life'. For most people 'work' is a massive part of their life. If vigorous, energetic, passionate workplaces exist (and they do, we've experienced them) then the question is: *How do we create them?*

Herein lies the value of this book. It's the missing link in leadership – the connection between past, present and a future so bright, you'll need to wear shades.

POP UP leadership

Cope, Martin & Peach 2018

Chapter 2

A TASTE OF LEADERSHIP

●●●●●●

In this chapter we acknowledge that there are some aspects of life in which size definitely does matter. Thankfully, leadership is not one and, indeed, we argue that small leadership might actually be better than super-sizing it?

We have a go at defining leadership, before franchising it out. Then we introduce Monica Seles as an unlikely leadership hero before moving onto pop-up leadership. Yes, we keep it brief, but pop-up is destined to be huge.

Then it's onto food: spaghetti and soup. Yummy!

We hope you're wearing your eating trousers? Let's tuck in …

How Big is Your 'L'?

It's important to distinguish between what we call 'BIG L' and 'little l' acts of leadership. Big acts of leadership ('BIG L') are strategic decisions and set piece meetings that you plan for. Company direction, restructures, takeovers, pricing, marketing campaigns, hiring and firing – these are all 'BIG L'.

......

'THE ESSENCE OF STRATEGY IS CHOOSING WHAT NOT TO DO.'

......

Michael Porter

'Big L' is important but it's not really what leadership is about. Neither is it what this book is about. 'Big L' is a series of epic projects that require strategic decisions. Real leadership is all about the 'little l' acts that affect the day-to-day climate in your team and, ultimately, your entire organization.

As a human being, you cannot NOT have an impact. Your 'little leadership' behaviours are setting the tone and it's often the smallest of 'little ls' that stamp your air of authenticity. This may sound trivial but it's the way you walk along the corridor – are you slouching and bleary eyed or head held high and smiling as you go? How do you stand in the lunchtime queue? Chatty and genuinely interested in your colleagues or aloof and scrolling on your phone? How do you look and what do you say when you enter the office on a dreary Monday morning? Do you stagger in, half-kempt, with a *'Morning all'* growl, or do you stride in purposefully and positively with the deliberate intent to set the tone?

There are some things that are so important they can be fitted into both the 'BIG L' and 'little l' categories. Werner Jensen, Michael Erhard and Steve Zaffron suggest integrity is 'a factor of production as important as knowledge or technology' and that integrity itself leads to incredible increases in performance.[10] Things like sticking to your word, smiling, listening, following through on promises, being on time and prepared in meetings, hitting deadlines and returning calls. No excuses that *something came up* or *the system was down* or *I cobbled it together at the last minute.*

We'll give you more of this later but suffice to say, in our gentle preamble, integrity slippage can cultivate indiscipline and inaction. Phrased more bluntly, it's just rank bad leadership example-setting.

Franchising Motivation

What then is 'leadership'? It's the theme of the book so it warrants a mention early on. 'Leadership' is such an important subject that it has its own genre in the bookstores. Celebs, football managers, gold medallists, business leaders, consultants, religious folk ... they've all had a go. There's such a wealth of information that you wonder why there are any rubbish leaders left in the world. And most, even the poor ones, get the theory. Listen to your staff, praise as much as possible, set SMART objectives, delegate (but don't over-delegate), *blah blah, yawn yawn.*

But, of course, leadership isn't a theory. It's not even a 'thing'. It's a feeling – an emotional connection. In modern parlance, it's akin to 'engagement'.

If you pick up 100 different leadership books you'll find 100 different nuanced definitions, most of which are dreadfully dull. So rather than attempt to provide yet another definition, we thought we'd provide some simplicity as to what leadership is and where it comes from.

Leadership is about getting people to go above and beyond their job description.

Simple as that! So whatever it is on that piece of paper that outlines, in black and white, what each person's job is ... your task is to get them to do more than that. There are various ways. You could follow the slackers around with a cattle-prod and every time they stop for a gossip give them a quick *'bzzzzt'*. Or, gotcha, checking Facebook in company time – *double bzzzzt!* However tempting that sounds, the chances are it would only work while you were in close proximity. The problem with punishment is that as soon as you're not looking, their productivity will decrease.

••••••

'LEADERSHIP ISN'T ABOUT WHAT HAPPENS WHEN YOU'RE THERE. IT'S ABOUT WHAT HAPPENS WHEN YOU'RE NOT.'

••••••

Anon

So, leaders beware! True leadership isn't about motivating your people. It's about showing your people how motivation rests with them individually and, thus, the team collectively. It's about what we call 'franchising' motivation – getting people to buy into the fact that motivation is theirs for the taking. A big part of your job is to help them make the right choices and, of course, you have to make good choices for yourself.

Pop-up Leadership

Seventeen-year-old Monica Seles burst onto the tennis scene in the 1990 French Open. At set point down to Steffi Graf, Seles' squeak became a grunt. As the grunt got louder, Seles went on to save three set points and win the match.

Now you might be thinking that's a weird story to include in a leadership book. And you'd be right, if it wasn't for the fact that nowadays, all tennis players grunt. Another example of the world's most excellent sheep.

Your organization can change its logo, revamp the website, pin values posters on the walls, re-structure the departments ... but they're all cosmetic. They're paying lip-service to change. The Monica Seles example gives you a clue as to one of the recurring themes of this book, that changing the behaviours of the leaders is what really matters. Leaders are copied. Fact. (Just to be clear, we're not advocating that you start grunting. Ours is a much broader concept around behavioural and emotional contagion. Standing at the photocopier, grunting? Well that'd just be scary.)

That means the positives as well as the negatives. The knee-wobbler is that ultimately, when you strip away the cosmetics and silence all the iffing and butting, your team is a reflection of you.

An organization cannot command employees to be happy and motivated – it's something that has to spread naturally throughout the organization. 'Group affective tone' is when emotions shared within the team are reproduced and reinforced by verbal and non-verbal behaviours – because emotions and the behaviours that go with them are contagious.[11] It is contagion which makes positive emotions an incredibly powerful tool in creating organizational cultures in which people can flourish.

We're going to introduce a super-cool way of thinking about leadership in the contemporary world.

Related to the above, we're calling it 'pop-up leadership'. This is leadership of the right type, in the right place at the right time. For example, sometimes your team is on steroids. If you're the leader, keep out of their bloody way. They're smashing productivity records left, right and centre. Other days, they need direction, or motivation, or coaching. Maybe praise, discipline or they just need to be allowed to go home early. The pop-up leader knows what's right. Moreover, the pop-up leader *does* what's right.

Pop-up leadership. Got it? Remember, you heard it here first.

Spaghetti and Soup

But wait, there's more ...

In *Connected*, Nicholas Christakis and James Fowler describe something they call the 'hyper-dyadic spread'. We call it 'attitudes are contagious'; the tendency of emotions to transmit from person to person, beyond an individual's direct ties.[12] They make the point almost poetically, describing the complex web of social connections thus: 'Ties do not extend outward in straight lines like spokes on a wheel. Instead these paths double back on themselves and spiral around like a tangled pile of spaghetti.' They found evidence to suggest that your emotions have a ripple effect that reaches three degrees of people removed from you. The magic numbers are 15, 10 and 6. If you've got a smile and a positive attitude, everyone with whom you come into direct contact experiences an emotional uplift of 15 per cent. That's terrific news because you're raising the emotional tone of your family, friends and work colleagues. But it doesn't stop there. Those 15 per cent happier folk then pass on their happiness to everyone they encounter, raising their levels by 10 per cent. Remember, you haven't actually met these 10 percenters directly but they have caught your happiness. And to complete the ripple, these 10 per cent happier folk pass your happiness on to everyone they meet by an extra 6 per cent.

But hang on a second. They're the stats for 'normal' people. You're a leader and Shawn Achor suggests 'the power to spark positive emotional contagion multiplies if you are in a leadership position' (p. 208).[13] Jennifer George and Kenneth Bettenhausen conclude that a positive leader engenders positive moods in their team, coordinating tasks better and with less effort[14] and Kim Cameron weighs in with the notion of positivity being analogous to the 'heliotropic effect': 'All living systems have an inclination towards the positive... plants lean towards the light...' (p xi).[15]

'Social referencing' describes the practice of taking one's cue from the leader. When a leader is in a positive mood, their positivity cascades down the organization and, according to Maureen Gaffney, 'this in turn makes them more optimistic about achieving their own goals, better at absorbing and understanding information, more creative and flexible and more effective as decision makers' (p. 251).[16]

You intuitively knew this anyway. Anthony Pescosolido[17] helps out by explaining how and why the leader creates an emotional ripple effect:

- Leaders typically talk more than team members and what they say is listened to more carefully.
- Leaders are often the first to speak and when others make comments their remarks frequently refer to what the leader has said.
- Because the leader's way of seeing things has extra weight, leaders 'manage meaning' for the group.
- Even when not talking, the leader is the most carefully watched member of a team.
- When team members raise questions for the group as a whole, most keep their eyes on the leader in order to gauge their response.
- Group members generally see the leader's emotional reaction as the most valid response, modelling their own on it (particularly in ambiguous situations).

Put simply, while every employee's emotions contribute to the overall mood of the team, leaders are *the most* contagious. Daniel Goleman calls it 'emotional soup', the analogy being that everyone is adding something to the team. A flavour, if you like. Two questions jump out; firstly, what flavours are you adding? Rhetorically, are they tasty ingredients like inspiration, positivity and energy, or are you inadvertently adding sarcasm, sighing and criticism? Secondly, not everyone is equal. Pescosolido's research states, unequivocally, that the leader has the biggest say in the flavour of the team soup!

Andy Cope, Mike Martin & Jonathan Peach

••••••

'BEING IN POWER IS LIKE BEING A LADY. IF YOU HAVE TO TELL PEOPLE YOU ARE, YOU AREN'T.'

••••••

Margaret Thatcher,
former British Prime Minister

All of a sudden, you begin to grasp the enormity of what we're talking about. It starts with you as a leader, but if you get the ingredients right, everyone benefits. So, our message is not to *'experiment with your impact'* or *'discover your power'* or *'seek to acquire more influence'*. It's much starker than that. The first rule of influence is that you already have it and, as a leader, it's multiplied.

The big question that we'll leave hanging for later is this: *If your emotions are highly infectious, what are your team members catching off you?*

Chapter 3
RELIGHT MY FIRE

●●●●●●

We start gently with the Green Cross Code and then ramp things up with an upper-cut from Mike Tyson. While you're still groggy, we explain why the world's best ever chapter on 'leadership history' has been consigned to the recycle bin.

Instead, we condense the age-old management/leadership ding-dong into one paragraph, set on horseback in the wild west of Wyoming. Like you would. We continue the softly-softly approach with Løgstrup and Radcliffe, the best authors never to appear on an MBA programme.

But beware. After lulling you in – BOOM – it all kicks off and before you know it, you're padded and helmeted for the Super Bowl where you're playing the game of your life. This, dear reader, is proper fast-paced rough stuff. Sprinting for all you're worth, we go from orange to green to Teal (and, yes, Teal needs a capital) and introduce you to the hardest thing to write about, the shift to organizations as living systems.

Just when you think you can't take any more, we take our foot off the gas by explaining why nobody ever cleans a rental car.

Confused? Excellent. Let's crack on …

The Best Chapter *Never* Written

......

'GETTING THROUGH LIFE IS LIKE THE GREEN CROSS CODE. SOMETIMES, BEFORE YOU STEP OFF THE KERB, IT'S BEST TO STOP, LOOK AND LISTEN.'

......

Unknown

Just so there's no pulling any wool over anyone's eyes, we wrote an entire chapter on leadership history, a glorious romp using the vehicle of *Bill & Ted's Excellent Adventure*. It was a cracking chapter full of fact, creativity and fun. In fact, I'd go so far as to suggest it was the best chapter of its kind ever written.

And we binned it.

Why? Because we love you and we value your time. Who really cares what was said and done 1000 years ago, or 50 years ago. Or even ten years ago? The quaint and relatively safe good old days have given way to the somewhat pacier think-on-your-feet-slightly-less-good new days.

Here's our cheat's guide to all you need to know about the evolution of leadership since the year dot.

- Leadership1.0 was doing the wrong thing, badly. Think Victorian factories. Lots of people died.
- Leadership 2.0 was doing the wrong thing, well. Think the forward thinkers of Victorian times – Cadbury, etc. They built communities and tidied up the workplaces. A bit. Fewer died.
- Leadership 3.0 was doing the right thing, wrong. *People are our most valuable resource* in mantra but not necessarily in practice. They half got it. Think 1980s. TQM, Balanced Score Card, servant leadership – leadership was bolted on as an afterthought.
- Leadership 4.0 was doing the right thing, but for the wrong reasons. Think banking culture. Empowerment, high motivation but totally profit driven, at the expense of customers.
- Leadership 5.0 is doing the right things for the right reasons. Oh, and doing them well. Guess what, that's where we're going ...

Every organization we work with goes to great lengths to explain the massive changes they're going through. It's usually a humungous restructure that involves new ways of thinking, collaborating and doing things that boils down to *we've got fewer people but we need greater output*. This might be okay if it was a one off, but it's happened so often that those doing the extra work are feeling increasingly hacked off.

This is normal. We'd be surprised if your organization is not going through something tumultuous. We're tipping well over to the wrong side of the classic time management curve, the 'distress' zone. Your body knows this and sooner or later it will send you a sign.

Wake up! Migraines, heart-burn and back pain aren't random occurrences, they're warning signals.

••••••

'EVERYONE HAS A PLAN UNTIL THEY'RE PUNCHED IN THE FACE.'

••••••

Mike Tyson

Stuff They Don't Tell You on an MBA (Yet)

The chapter that we binned was a true marvel, showcasing the work of the management greats. In the end, there were two we couldn't cut.

Unless you're a leadership geek, you have probably never heard of Danish philosopher K.E. Løgstrup.[18] Here's the basic gist of his most influential idea, presented in 1965: trust is not of our own making; it is given. Life cannot be lived without one person laying him or herself open to another person and putting themselves into that person's hands.

You might have to read that a couple of times? The kernel of the message is that we help to shape another person's world by our attitude towards them. Our attitude becomes a lens through which they live their life and, indeed, our attitude to others becomes ultra-powerful: it helps to determine the size and colour of their world; we make it large or small, bright or drab, rich or dull, threatening or secure. The whole point is we help to shape their world, not by complicated theories, but by our own attitude towards them.

We think this applies in every aspect of life but, work-wise, we often get bogged down in other concerns and our attitude towards those around us is affected by pressures of time, performance and resources. You are pressured so, naturally, you push towards the targets and take your eye off the people. But it doesn't matter what types of pressure your job brings – none of it gives you licence to treat other people with less than utmost respect and care. This principle is doubly important for managers, whose bad and/or insipid behaviour is observed by employees and adopted as the new norm. And at that point everything starts to unravel.

In short, while Løgstrup's 'ethical demand' has become a lot harder to live by in modern workplaces, it is as important as ever. Perhaps more so in today's pressured world.

Andy Cope, Mike Martin & Jonathan Peach

••••••

'THE BEST THING YOU CAN DO IS GET GOOD AT BEING YOU.'

••••••

Dennis T. Menace

As we said, these seeds were sown several decades ago. It sometimes takes a while for a way of thinking to embed. It needs a time and place, which we reckon is right about now. Løgstrup's idea isn't that leadership is about a 'great person', a 'situation' or a 'transformation' – it's simply that we need to be true and authentic, pitching in at the top end of who we already are. So, less about trying to be someone else, and more about being yourself, brilliantly.

Another thoroughly modern gem is Steve Radcliffe's concept of FED (Future – Engage – Deliver),[19] which shares Løgstrup's core themes and brings them bang up to date. Brace yourself for some simplicity: when you're being yourself, brilliantly, you are glowing with creativity, positivity and ideas. You are in tune with what you care about and where you're going. Best of all, you inspire others. And, of course, being your best self doesn't mean you won't hit setbacks or roadblocks or idiots. You'll come face to face with apathy and resistance but you'll be creative in how you handle them. You, at your best, are bestowed with oodles of bouncebackability and you'll have more uptime than downtime.

······

'MAKING IT UP AS YOU GO ALONG IS A GOOD PLAN.'

······

Ian Gilbert

In line with what we said earlier, Radcliffe's 'thing' is that leadership is about what you're like and how you come across, not what techniques or processes you've got. FED suggests leadership is not about competencies, skills or personality. It's not about inspiring people or trying to motivate them. It's about being inspired. Radcliffe points out that inspiration comes from being in touch with your passion and then going for it. So, in FED, Radcliffe's first base is to ask yourself: *What do I care about?* So, go on, ask yourself: what matters to you? What do you value the most? What lights your internal fire? The truth is that it might have nothing to do with work.

Radcliffe's second base is to ask: *What do you want to lead for?* How cool a question is that? If we were to ask in a slightly different way that linked to first base it might be: *What specifically do you want to make happen that is part of what you care about?*

The modern bandwagon might call Løgstrup's idea something like 'authentic leadership theory' and it's working its way through some tricky growing pains. We think FED has fed it (so to speak) by putting it into a modern context.

It's OK to Corral

There are other books that expend entire chapters on the 'leadership' versus 'management' debate. We're very keen not to write just any old book, so our take is summarized in the metaphor below.

If you watch the black and white cowboy movies, they were invariably set on a ranch, a vast chunk of rugged Wyoming, in which the cattle can roam freely. Except of course they can't. The ranch has invisible boundaries and every so often the cowboys set out to corral their livestock. The point is they enjoy freedom *within* limits. In organizational terms, management sets the boundaries. Leadership seeks to engage employees to the point whereby they can accomplish as much as possible *within* the boundaries.

Now it's important to operate in the real world here – it's not simply a case of saying management is dead, long live leadership. We need a balance of both – and the right balance depends on you, your team, your organization and the context you are all operating within. But we need to take care because swinging the balance too far across to management will corral your people well within their limits. The converse is a swing too far towards some sort of laissez-faire leadership where the boundaries are lost and your people are wandering aimlessly.

The sheer speed of life is making organizations change faster than ever just to stay in the game. We think that maybe the needs of most organizations have developed well beyond the limits imposed by their management model, so even those considered 'good' in the past may be getting in the way of their own success.

Remember we told you that we'd binned a whole chapter on the history of leadership thinking? We're less interested in looking at leadership through the rear-view mirror and much more eyes forward. So buckle up and eyes on the road ahead. We're going to show you a glimpse of what's around the next bend ...

You'll Needing Shoulder Pads and Running Shoes

······

'THE MOST EXCITING BREAKTHROUGHS OF THE 21ST CENTURY WILL NOT OCCUR BECAUSE OF TECHNOLOGY, BUT BECAUSE OF AN EXPANDING CONCEPT OF WHAT IT MEANS TO BE HUMAN.'

······

John Naisbitt

Imagine a workplace that was engaging and fun? Suspend your disbelief just for a second and consider what the workplace would be like if, at the end of the working day, your employees were more energized than when they logged on? So, rather than draining them, work invigorated them?

It's an interesting notion. The question is: *How?*

None of us really understand American football. We're not sure anybody does? The bit we *do* get is that the quarterback is a key player, as are the wide receivers. The quarterback's job is not to throw the ball directly to the wide receiver, but to throw the ball to where the wide receiver is *going to be.*

So for this next section, we're going to play quarterback and you're the fleet-footed wide receiver. Helmet secured? Off you go, that-a-way ...

Let's zip you through some colours, as suggested by Frederic Laloux.[20] Orange organizations are traditional, often described as 'mechanistic'. If they still exist at all, they're taking on water, *Titanic*-style, their inappropriateness for the modern world plain for all to see. Managers still do the thinking and workers do the working. The lifeboats are mustered and the clever folk are already abandoning ship.

······

'ANY COMPANY DESIGNED FOR SUCCESS IN THE 20TH CENTURY IS DOOMED TO FAILURE IN THE 21ST.'

······

David Rose

Most organizations have done what expensive consultants told them to do and set about creating nice places to spend your day. These so-called green organizations have made the necessary changes, shimmying up the evolutionary scale to equip themselves for the here and now of the modern world. They've done the empowerment and self-managed teams thing. Decisions have been pushed down to those in the trenches with the thinking that they're closer to the mud so they'll know what needs doing. Managers are tasked with giving up power and becoming 'servant leaders'. Their job is to listen, empower, motivate and coach.

It works. A bit. Sometimes. Quite often, despite what the organization espouses, the reality felt by employees is the opposite. So, while managers talk a good talk, the feeling of those with their faces in the mud is one of no purpose, spartan resources, managers making all the decisions while they're up to their eyeballs in shit.

Example? Looking through the eyes of a care worker with a list of 30 appointments that she knows she can't do, that's been put together by a planner she's never met, with clients she doesn't know – her day starts badly, and goes downhill from there.

So what colour comes next?

At the radical end of the organizational design spectrum is work on so-called Teal organizations. There's a big fat chance that you've never heard that term before, but we think it will be coming on stream in the next few years.

Fact of the day

Women have superior brains and something called 'retrachromic vision'. It enables them to distinguish between colours that men just don't see. All men see in only 16 colours. 'Watermelon', for example, is a fruit, not a colour. So is 'Pumpkin'.

And we have no idea what 'mauve' is. Ditto Teal.

Thank you.

For the men, teal is a colour, pitched somewhere between green and blue.

The Teal paradigm also applies to the modern world of work and is more aligned to human consciousness than traditional organizational thinking. Command and control, hierarchies, service level agreements, job descriptions, all the traditional staples of the last 150 years are swept away. People's actions are guided not by orders from someone up the chain of command but by 'listening' to the organization's purpose.

Teal is characterized by rapid change and adaptation, as adjustments are continuously made to better serve the organization's purpose.

Hang in there. Before you dismiss its greeny-blueyness as pink and fluffy, remember you're still metaphorically sprinting to where the organizational ball's *going to be*. (I hadn't realized how difficult this was to write about until I started writing about it. Trying to make Teal sound anything other than maverick, that is.)

Traditional organizations have always been places that encourage people to show up with a narrow 'professional' self and to check other parts of your persona at the door. Historically, they've been about masculine resolve, displays of determination and strength, and hiding doubts and vulnerability. Rationality and a cool business head have been the order of the day, while the emotional, intuitive, and spiritual parts of ourselves often feel unwelcome and out of place.

Teal organizations are about 'wholeness' as well as purpose. There are a few trailblazers who've developed a set of practices that invite us to reclaim our inner wholeness and bring all of who we are to work.

Teals are seen as having a life and a sense of direction of their own. Instead of trying to predict and control the future, members of the organization are invited to listen in and understand what the organization wants to become, what purpose it wants to serve. Laloux daringly suggests it's as if '... *somebody put a billion dollars into your psychological account*'.

......

'WHEN YOU CHANGE THE WAY YOU LOOK AT THINGS, THE THINGS YOU LOOK AT CHANGE.'

......

Wayne Dyer

Teal organizations refer to themselves as living systems. Life consists of ecosystems, each separate, yet inextricably connected. Change in nature happens everywhere, all the time, in a self-organizing urge that comes from every cell and every organism. There's no need for central command and control to give orders or pull nature's levers.

The simplest analogy I can give you (and I'm doing Teal a dis-service by doing so) is that Teal is an extension of total quality management. This 1960s movement revolutionized quality by making it everyone's responsibility, essentially building quality into the fabric of the organization. That's crazy, right? You'd have to trust people on the shop floor to *want* to do a fabulous job.

While the British manufacturers limped along with their outdated production lines where 'quality control' was vested in a team of inspectors, the Japanese sprinted ahead. No inspectors were needed. British manufacturing struggled to compete and all but closed down. Now it's crazy not to be doing TQM.

Teal takes this concept beyond quality, into leadership, thinking, creativity, purpose and even consciousness. If 'leadership' is everyone's responsibility then you don't need leaders. I know. It's supposed to scare you. It's your classic 'turkeys don't vote for Christmas'. Leaderless organizations? We'd be designing ourselves out of a job. And it'd be anarchy, right?

Perhaps? Time will tell. The American 'leadership football' is still in the air. We think it's worth positioning yourself for where it's heading.

> Fact
>
> *Baby eagles learn to fly by being pushed out of the nest. They have 500 feet to learn!*

We'll come back to Teal in the final chapter. Meantime, an easier way to think about Teal is to reflect that, at some point, you will have rented a car. Most likely, this will have been on holiday. So, here's a question for you: *before you returned the car to the airport, did you wash it?*

Why on earth not?

Because it's not yours, that's why. To be truthful, you probably didn't treat it very well either.

Bringing the concept to your team – are your people 'renting' or 'owning'? Organizations that achieve ownership will be rewarded with genuine and loving care.

Teal? It's about owning.

Chapter 4

JOINING THE DOTS

● ● ● ● ● ●

We like to think all our chapters are epic but 4 and 5 are our 'Ben Hur': grand in scale, out of control, over budget but (we think) worthy of awards. This is where we wake up from the donkey derby of 'job satisfaction' and chariot race into the cut and thrust of 'job engagement'.

We're all for change but we find someone's gone and moved Australia? This is change madness, because if you shift Oz, everything else moves too. We give you the world's shortest poem and from then on it's rabbits, ducks and diversity … I mean, what's not to like?

We've always been a bit jealous of education and its 3Rs so, in a mind-blowing explosion of simplicity, we've supplanted the Rs to leadership.

There's a lot more besides, but this chapter is basically a PhD, but without the 'P', 'h' or 'D'. Is it possible to dumb academia down to the level of a children's story?

Are you sitting comfortably? Then let's begin …

Connecting the Disconnected

······

'IT'S EASY TO GET GOOD PLAYERS. GETTING THEM TO PLAY TOGETHER, THAT'S THE HARD PART.'

······

Casey Stengel

Challenging yourself to be your best self is first base. Your day can slip and most of us find it pretty easy to justify when we've had a bad day – excessive workload, lack of sleep, bad traffic, surrounded by idiots, etc.

However, we're less understanding with others. Indeed, we can be very quick to have a pop at someone else when they don't behave in the way we think they should. The thing is we sometimes expect others, particularly our bosses, to behave in a way that they may not even be capable of, yet we are continually surprised and disappointed when they fail to meet the expectations we have set in our minds about them. It's worth remembering that just because your boss isn't living up to your expectations, that doesn't make him or her a bad person. Unless, of course, your boss is systematically torturing hostages chained to the walls in their cellar, which would probably indicate that they are lacking in empathy as a leader as well as being a bad person.

Top Tip

Never waste a crisis.

The more crises that come our way, the more we can be excused for throwing ourselves headlong at the problem(s). I mean, after all, when everyone around you is sinking, the right thing to do is roll up your sleeves and muck in, right?

Maybe. It can be easy to get sucked into helping out at the coalface. Jumping in, superhero-like, is sometimes absolutely the right thing to do. We've devoted the whole of Chapter 9 to superheroes but while we're on the theme, we may as well clear up a couple of matters right now.

Firstly, you need to understand that not all superheroes wear capes. Some might wear a headset, a hard hat, tabard, overalls or a tool belt. Transport-wise, while a Batmobile might be ultra-cool, it's more likely your superheroes will drive a van, a lorry or turn up at work in an ordinary car. Incredibly, some superheroes actually cycle to work. And while the movies might have you believe in a lasso of truth or invisibility cloak, your real-life superheroes might wield a mop and bucket spanner, keyboard, spreadsheet or ordinary looking briefcase. So superhero lesson #1: just because your team members look normal, doesn't mean there's not a superhero inside, itching to get out.

Second, spotting them is the easy part. Getting your Diana Princes and Peter Parkers to reveal themselves to the world is not always as easy as it seems. Remember, they might not actually know? Or they simply forgot they were amazing? Recall the first Harry Potter movie. Our speccy hero was living in cramped conditions underneath the stairs. He had no idea that he was a wizard! Indeed, it took a while for him to start believing in himself.

Thirdly, if points 1 and 2 are about reminding you that leadership isn't about being a superhero, it's about *creating* them, there must be a more subtle leadership point underpinning everything we're saying, and it's probably this:

Superhero lesson #3 is that *however much you like the feeling of cape, tight lycra and pants on the outside, continuing to haul your team out of the mire won't help in the long run.*

So what's the real answer? If you're being an inspirational leader, the best version of you, what should you be focussing on? Should you be making a passionate authentic speech from the balcony? Should you be explaining the intricacies of your magnificent vision, telling the stories that help them make meaning of it? Should you be leading the charge with your sabre in the air (this is not a euphemism).

We believe the best place to start is with connection. Martin Luther King got it just about right. How did he start the civil rights revolution? Did he stand on the steps of the Lincoln Memorial and announce, *'I have a set of service level agreements and a strategic plan'*? Err, no. His impassioned *'I have a dream ...'* speech brought to bear three things: connection, potential and reason. Mr King started a civil rights movement by articulating a dream. The good doctor had a passion for change.

Connection is massively important. How often have you seen a national sports team that, on paper, would be unbeatable? The very best player in the country in every position. Yet sometimes you know that their club team, with only a few of those players, would play better, because they're just a bunch of high performing individuals with no real connection. An inspired leader will ensure they are connected with their team and, just as importantly, the team are connected with each other. Yes, it is as challenging as it sounds, but it's worth it. Connection is the making, or breaking of a team.

Getting up to Something, *Together*

Muhammad Ali addressed the graduating class at Harvard in 1975. The champ was known for coming up with clever poems, so an audience member asked him to recite one and, at a length of exactly two words, what followed may very well be the shortest poem in recorded history. Ali said:

'*Me, We.*'

It's a pithy reminder of the importance of empathy. Introspection only gets you so far. We need some 'outrospection' to really live good lives.

David Sirota, Louis Mischkind and Michael Meltzer[21] suggest that three factors are critical in producing a happy and enthusiastic workforce. First of all, 'equity' and for equity read respectful and dignified treatment, fairness and security. Next, 'achievement', which includes an array of factors such as pride in the organization, empowerment, feedback and the Goldilocks amount of job challenge. Thirdly, and often missed in other leadership books, 'camaraderie with one's work colleagues'. High-quality connections are important sources of happiness and energy for employees, with Tom Rath[22] reporting that individuals who have a bestie at work are seven times more likely to be engaged in their job.

Management gurus used to advocate MBWA (Management By Walking About): a call to arms that required managers to forcibly remove their backsides from their desks and walk the floor, chatting, smiling, listening, building relationships, being present, praising, encouraging, catching staff doing things right, making eye contact, being available. The Japanese have a similar concept: Gemba – a place where value is created – meaning the leader ought to be where the people are working so he or she can get an understanding of how it's going.

Nowadays, teams are so dispersed that it might be MBFA (Management By Flying Around) or MBSA (Management By Skyping Around) – it's a modern morphing of the same point. Being visible.

Recently, Andy visited the offices of a well-known organization whose swanky open-plan office contained 3000 people. And, guess what, the boss's desk is slap bang in the thick of it. She doesn't have the corner office with the fridge, minibar, couch and city view, she is part of the team.

Gemba, at its best.

Taking connectedness and motivation to the next level, here are Gallup's tried and tested questions.[23] If your staff are affirmative in all these, you're not going far wrong.

1 Do I know what is expected of me at work?
2 Do I have the materials and equipment I need to do my work right?
3 At work, do I have the opportunity to do what I do best every day?
4 In the last seven days, have I received recognition or praise for doing good work?
5 Does my supervisor, or someone at work, seem to care about me as a person?
6 Is there someone at work who encourages my development?
7 At work, do my opinions seem to count?
8 Does the mission/purpose of my company make me feel my job is important?
9 Are my co-workers committed to doing quality work?
10 Do I have a best friend at work?
11 In the last six months, has someone at work talked to me about my progress?
12 This last year, have I had opportunities at work to learn and grow?

Surrounded by Idiots?

Jane Dutton[24] speaks of 'high-quality connections' (HQC) which give a sense of heightened energy. In HQCs, people feel attuned to each other and experience a sense of mutuality and positive regard as well as feeling a sense of worth and value. Barbara Fredrickson[25] purports that these moments of connection start people on an upward spiral of growth and fulfilment.

Nice. Lovely in fact. But what about the idiots?

If your internal dialogue through the day is made up of *I see idiots* with a good smattering of *have some lost the plot?* and a healthy dose of *WTF?*, we're pretty sure there's a disconnect with your team, and there's a word for that – *normal.*

> Today's challenge
>
> *Don't fire poor performers. Fire them up.*

Getting everyone on board and motivated all day every day is perhaps the biggest leadership challenge of all. First up, don't be too hard on yourself. You can't cure stupid. Sorry if that sounds harsh, but you might inherit a team member (or two) who are just not up to it and, what's more, they never will be. (BTW, have you noticed how idiots always seem to have opinions opposite to your own? Weird that.)

If, on the other hand, you're surrounded by idiots, the uncomfortable truth is it's more likely that you are. Sorry about that. We could have 'bad news sandwiched' that one with a *nice hair* and a *love the shoes* but, as we'll be telling you to dump that concept in Chapter 6, we thought we'd just go for it.

This is not to say that you don't have nice shoes or great hair of course. Let's stop digging and move on and explain ...

Mood hoover's special talent...

He is bi-lingual: he speaks both Bullshit and Bollocks

If, like your authors, you remember the great 80s quiz show *Catchphrase*, take a quick look at the picture below and as Roy Walker would say, *'Say what you see'*.

Be honest, what did you see first – the duck, obviously.

Or, hang on, maybe you saw the rabbit?

Seeing the duck or rabbit first doesn't say anything about you or your mental wellbeing. We were just illustrating that two people can look at the same thing and take something different from it. Oh, and by the way, if you can see a barren post-apocalyptic landscape strewn with the skulls of humanity with a flying demon about to feast on our burned remains, please put the book down now and make an emergency appointment with your doctor.

That's the thing about people. We think differently. In his book *The Element*, Sir Ken Robinson talks about the Myers Briggs personality types and suggests that a model which shoehorns us into 16 different personality types is somewhat limited. He suggests that the number is more akin to whatever the current population of earth stands at. That's why we can explain our strategy and plan to our team and they can walk away with different interpretations of it. That's why we can get frustrated when people don't 'get it' and why so many find it hard to connect.[26]

Here's a lovely story …

A young couple moved into a swanky apartment in a new neighbourhood. They sat in their kitchen having breakfast, watching the world go by. The woman saw her neighbour pegging out the washing. 'That laundry's not very clean,' she tutted. 'She either needs a new washing machine or better washing powder.'

Other than the crunching on his toast, her husband remained silent.

His wife's comment was exactly the same the next day. And the next. 'Why on earth is that woman hanging out dirty washing?' she sighed in disgust. 'She needs lessons in basic hygiene!'

And her husband crunched, knowingly.

On the fourth day his wife plonked herself at the breakfast table with a gleeful smile. 'At last,' she said, pointing at their neighbour's washing line. Her husband followed her gaze to the neatly arranged clothes line where the whites sparkled and the colours shone. 'All of a sudden she seems to have learned to clean properly.'

And her husband broke his silence. 'I got up early this morning and cleaned our windows.'

Let's get a fresh perspective by diverting to one of Andy's 'asides', a true story from 1993... (Yes, he's used it in a previous book but it's good enough to use again. Thank you.)

It was early morning as we touched down in Australia. Bleary eyed, I grabbed a taxi to a youth hostel and tucked into a bowl of cornflakes and fresh milk. Three months in South-east Asia meant that a non-rice meal was greedily guzzled. Eventually, I removed my chin from the bowl and looked around. There was a huge world map on the wall. I did a double take. Australia was in the middle. How bizarre.

The tectonic plates had shifted. The UK was still a tiny outcrop but shunting Oz to centre stage had moved us to top left, where America should be. And America had popped up on the right. I pondered that map for quite a while without realizing I would end up writing about it thirty years later.

In the intervening period, the internet was born, quickly followed by the Google Maps app. For the uninitiated, you open the app and it tells you where you are. You are a blue dot. You can then tap in where you'd like to go and Google will plot a route and you can walk along, following the progress of the blue dot you.

Rather like the Australians putting themselves in the centre of their world, the blue dot is how you live your life. You are, quite naturally, focused on yourself. Sure, you look out for others but, as we've explained, the world is processed and interpreted by you. You are the centre of your universe. And because of the way your mind works, you sort of assume that you are the centre of everybody else's universe too. But, of course, you're not. Everybody is their own blue dot, the epicentre of their own world.

We see, hear, taste, touch and smell in the only way we can. As ourselves. That means you and I live on the same planet as billions of other people, but we don't all live in the same world. Every one of us perceives the world around us differently because we have different brain filters. We can only ever experience the world as our own blue dot.

When you think of it like that, you can see why people (those you may formerly have labelled as idiots) don't always agree with you. At a basic level, connection is easy with those who think like we do. We've got lots in common, we hold similar views and most importantly we rarely make each other wrong. Academia has got some labels for it, like 'halo effect' and 'confirmation bias' as it sounds a lot better than 'our brain filters are similar'.

When you have different sets of filters it takes a bit more effort and, once you realize it's just that 'they view the world differently to me', it gets easier. It also gets more interesting when you get that their view of the world adds value to yours because they come up with insights that your brain filters out.

You've experienced teams with varying levels of connection and you know that a connected team is a joy to work in, while a disconnected one makes the working week a bloody nightmare. You also know that the best place to find the things we are lacking is within those who are different from us.

The secret of *how* to connect is often over-complicated and over-blown to the point where the answer disappears up its own backside. So please allow us to simplify. Sit back and relax while we give you an answer so simple that a five-year-old could understand it.

In fact, brace yourself, I can feel a children's story coming on ...

Mister Nobody and the Silver Bullet

There's an awful lot written about employee motivation and, yes, a lot of it is *awful* – over-complicated 'self-actualization', 'operant', 'cognitive dissonance', 'intrinsic/extrinsic' babble. It's 50 shades of unnecessary pain. If you want to be tied up and beaten with a riding crop before we reveal the glorious truth, that's fine. Go get into your gimp mask but you'll have to self-flagellate or phone a friend.

We don't deal in pain.

As is our way, our story of connection starts in Trafalgar Square, London. As well as a contributor to this magnificent book, Andy is a children's author and had been invited to the capital to do a book signing. While that sentence might be good for his ego, the next sentence kills it. A grand total of zero (nil, null, zilch, none, the big 0) children turned up to buy one of his books and, crimson faced, he spent an hour in the children's section of Waterstones, flagship store trying to hide his humiliation. He absorbed himself in the *Mr Men* series, checking if there was a *Mr Embarrassed* or maybe a *Mr Curl-Up-In-The-Corner-And-Die*? There wasn't but, as luck would have it, there was something much more excruciating, a brand-new *Mr Men* book which Andy picked from the shelf and read, cover to cover.

Mr Nobody is the saddest children's book ever written. Let me regale you with the basics. Mr Nobody is sobbing his heart out when along comes Mr Happy. He hears Mr Nobody, a sort of *'somebody who was but wasn't'* and asks him what's wrong.

Mr Nobody wails that he is a nobody. Even worse, he knew he used to be a somebody, but he can't remember who.

Ever chipper, Mr Happy's grin remains fixed and he offers to help but Mr Nobody is steadfast in the belief that, 'There's nothing you can do about a nobody.'

'*Of course there is*' said Mr Happy. '*Follow me.*'

They say everything happens for a reason. That story, gut-wrenching as it is, was the real reason I was in London. It was the moment when everything clicked. I had a degree in Management, a Masters in Leadership and a PhD in Flourishing and yet, here it was, disguised as a children's book. Thousands of parents had read Mr Nobody's story to their children, not realizing that it was the best leadership tale ever.

The book was so bad, I bought it and on the train home, I re-Googled the Gallup survey questions from earlier. As we rattled through Kidderminster, I found it. *I was right!* There was a statement that, if you can tick 'agree', has clear implications for feeling great at work. The statement is this:

'*My supervisor, or someone at work, seems to care about me as a person.*'

After studying proper academia for 20 years (I describe myself as a 'recovering academic'), this statement took the wind out of me. '*Someone at work seems to care about me as a person*'. Could that be it? Could it really be so simple? Could Mr Happy's genuine concern for his flailing colleague actually be the silver bullet of connection?

Well, we're not claiming it's quite that simple, but it's certainly a massive clue. Chances are, you already genuinely care about your people but the deeper question is how can you demonstrably care, even more? Putting it another way, it's all well and good *you* knowing you care about your people, *but do they know?*

This *Mr Men* notion takes us down the cul-de-sac of simplicity, where all roads lead to the same concept, something that we're calling the 3Rs of motivation: relationships, relationships and (you've guessed it) *relationships*.

We told you it was obvious! But between us we have 100 years of experience of working in organizations and we promise you, common sense doesn't always tally with common practice.

Oh, and by the way, it's 'little l', all the way!

The Social Network

True. Always.

In high performance teams, the members aren't just committed to the success of the team; they are also committed to the success of each other.

Pretty much forever, 'organizational behaviour' (an umbrella term that includes motivation, leadership, teams and culture, among others) was about measuring and reporting on 'employee satisfaction'. The mantra was that the organization needed to contort itself in such a way as to create the ideal conditions for staff to feel 'satisfied'. There are various definitions of 'job satisfaction' but they all point to the same underlying issue – it implies a fairly passive experience.

Being 'satisfied' with your job means you believe it has provided (or will provide) an acceptable level of what is wanted, putting it on par with achieving a level of comfort or adequacy rather than a state of dynamism. And that's fine, if you want mediocrity. So, if the mission statement emblazoned on your office wall reads *To be like everyone else* or *Striving to be bog standard*, read no further.

David Taylor sends up the concept of 'satisfactory' hilariously in one of his blogs. He suggests that you should imagine a romantic evening during which your partner has cooked a meal. You chomp your way through the courses and when they ask if you enjoyed it, you say, *'It met my expectations'*. If (and it's a very big 'if') after the meal, one thing leads to another and you end up sitting in bed, lighting the post-coital cigar, and your partner dreamily asks, *'How was it for you?'* – puffing a smoke ring and purring *'satisfactory'* may well end your relationship.

It was only very recently that we began to question the assumption that 'job satisfaction' is the right utopia to be aiming for. 'Satisfied' is equated with 'adequacy' and that's hardly aspiring to world class.

Enter, centre stage, 'engagement'. *Ta daa!* [imagine a wolf whistle]. But if we put engagement centre stage and shine a dazzling light in its eyes, would it bear scrutiny?

First up, it's closely related to the concept of 'thriving at work' in which employees experience feelings of vitality and energy with beliefs that they are learning, developing and making progress towards being their best self.[27] Arnold

Bakker and Evangelia Demerouti describe engagement as, 'a positive, fulfilling, work-related state of mind that is characterized by vigour, dedication and absorption'.[28]

Bakker[29] suggests several reasons why engagement improves performance. Engaged employees more likely to agree with statements such as, '*I eat, live and breathe my job*', '*At my work, I feel bursting with energy*', '*I find the work that I do full of meaning and purpose*', and '*When I am working, I forget everything else around me*'.

Even better news – engaged employees spread enthusiasm. In Wayne Baker, Rob Cross and Melissa Wooten's study,[30] energizing relationships produced feelings of being 'stimulated', 'up', 'intense' and 'animated'. Employees explained how energizing relationships made them feel engrossed, enthused and drawn in. But feelings were only the beginning – behaviours supporting the organization came hot on their heels, including willingness to devote discretionary time to work issues. In modern business parlance that's akin to '*going the extra mile*' or, to use our definition of leadership from earlier, '*going above your job description*'.

Bottom line? *Engagement is the bottom line!*

We hope you can see why we're so excited? This goes way above 'satisfaction' into high levels of energy and resilience, way above 'acceptable' into being fully present and happily engrossed – the psychological state of 'flow' where time passes quickly and you are totally absorbed in your work. Crucially, when 'in flow' your productivity goes through the roof but you feel energized rather than drained. It's a state in which you're challenged in just the way you like to be challenged.

It's hard to argue with Simon Sinek's assertion that leadership is not about being in charge but about *taking care of those in your charge*.[31]

So this chapter has been a halfway house. It's been about connecting the dots – next up, how to get the dots to be inspired ...

"It took Andy C 12 years to cotton on!"

Chapter 5

ONE FOR THE GROWN-UPS

••••••

Chapters 4 and 5 are like Christmas dinner – yummy, but way too much in one sitting. So, rather than leaving you feeling bloated, we suggest you go for some fresh air to 'walk off' Chapter 4 and make room for Chapter 5. Oh, and continuing the festive theme, we suggest a way of feeding your entire street next Christmas.

This is the only section of the book that you might need to read two or three times before the concepts and magnitude sinks in. We lighten things up by getting to grips with 'mood hoovers' and '2 percenters' and we explain why Tigger hasn't got any friends.

In a book that is crammed with happiness and positivity, we are about to suggest, somewhat counter-intuitively, that you create slightly less happiness.

Odd?

Good!

'It's life Jim, but not as we know it.'

Following on from Chapter 4 (or, if you prefer to use your American box-set voice, try *'Previously, in Chapter 4 ...'*) we explained that placid states like 'employee satisfaction' mean employees' wants are just about being fulfilled. If you want a technical term, satisfied employees are a bit *meh*.

> Definition
>
> **Meh:** *Expressing a lack of interest or enthusiasm. Uninspiring. Unexceptional. A verbal shrug.*

'Job satisfaction' sets the motivational bar very low whereas 'engagement' requires one of Dick Fosbury's bar-raising flops. Andy's research shows that in activated states like engagement, individuals still have wants that are unsatisfied. Engaged staff are actually experiencing a kind of *dissatisfied happiness*. Things are OK, but they are striving for them to be better.

Examples abound. Here's one. I was driving behind a white van (I'll call the business 'Rainbow Solutions') when a cigarette butt and several empty crisp packets were ejected from the passenger window. The back doors were filthy and someone had drawn in the dirt with their finger. On the left door was a sad face, underneath it was written 'Monday'. On the right door was a smiley face, underneath it was written

'Friday'! Straight-mouthed Wednesday was sandwiched in-between.

It made me wonder why on earth would I give 'Rainbow Solutions' a call on any day other than a Friday? And what would happen if they turned up to a job at my house on a Monday?

The difference between benign 'satisfaction' and active 'engagement' is incredibly important for modern-day leadership. What follows might be a paragraph for the organizational behavioural purists but we hope you'll hang in there. Most studies of job satisfaction have been examined in terms of person-environment fit, meaning that incompatibility between an individual and their environment is viewed as a significant source of stress – not a driver for growth. So, ever since organizations were invented, we have been tinkering with their design to give employees what we think they want to be 'satisfied' at work. In doing so everything becomes the same shade of grey. We've accidentally built 'adequacy' into our workplaces which explains why everyone's feeling a bit *meh*.

Fosbury-flopping yourself over the bar at world record level requires individuals to be 'ok' in the here and now, but also driven by wanting things to be better. Engaged employees are driven with vigour and energy. In short, they are not ok with 'ok'.

The fact that employee engagement can be linked with unsatisfied wants seems counter-intuitive to traditional studies. It's almost (but not quite) suggesting that organizations should stop striving to create fabulous working environments. On balance, it would probably be a bad move to take away the restaurant, water cooler, vending machine, gym, dress-down Friday and cigarette breaks. As Joanne Gavin and Richard Mason state, 'In order to achieve the good life people must work in good organizations' (p. 387).[32] Nigel Marsh chips in, suggesting bad companies are 'the abattoirs of the human soul'.[33] Ouch! But very true.

Our point is so much bigger. The conditions above are all well and good, *but not enough to secure engagement*. Creating a decent working environment is first base. You can think of people who work in super environments, with a pool table in the staffroom, a fruit bowl in the office and free massages at their desks, and yet steadfastly refuse to be engaged at work.

Engagement, you see, is a symbiotic relationship between the organization *and* the person. Let's take another peep at Andy's research. He measured employee emotions and mapped them to create a pretty spider diagram of employees' feelings.

Why not have a go and see if you can prove something to yourself. Think about your last working week, get a pen and map yourself against the 16 emotions. Keep it rough and ready – gauging the percentage of time you experienced each one.

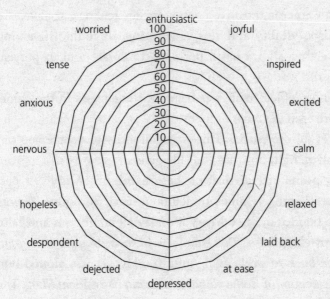

For your information, the top right quadrant's emotions (enthusiastic, joyful, inspired and excited) are summarized as 'engaged'. The bottom quadrant's emotions (calm, relaxed, laid back and at ease) are 'satisfied'. Bottom left (depressed, dejected, despondent and hopeless) are labelled as 'depression' and top left (nervous, anxious, tense and worried) are aggregated together as 'anxiety'.

So what?

Well, Andy's research graphed employees onto the diagram so he built up a heat map of workplace emotions. The white-hot stuff is happening in the top right quadrant, a space inhabited by what Andy calls '2 percenters'. These employees are not only significantly happier but they also possess bags more energy. Tying in to the fabulous work of

Kim Cameron, positive energy creates feelings of aliveness, arousal, vitality and zest, suggesting, 'It is the life-giving force that allows us to perform, to create and to persist' (p. 49).[34]

The problem with '2 percenters'? The clue's in the name. There aren't enough of them!

Yet they're crucial. This small minority of people you can think of, right now, are your life-givers.

A point of clarification before the off, Andy's '2 percenters' aren't a bunch of self-nominated corporate Tiggers who bounce in on a dreary Monday all jazz-hands and false happy-clappiness. *'Don't those weekends drag. Isn't it great to be back to work!'* will, quite frankly, get you slotted into the category of *'some village is missing its resident idiot'*. The '2 percenters' have been painstakingly sought and filtered through various processes, the most important of which is that they have been nominated by others in the organization as *someone at work who makes me feel good*. So, yes, they rate very high on happiness and energy but, crucially, their feel-good factor has leaked.

Why Vitality is so Vital

With that cleared up, we can go back to Kim Cameron. His work on organizational vitality examines four types of energy; physical, mental, psychological and relational – only one of which is renewable.

Physical energy is the body's naturally occurring energy, produced by burning calories. Psychological energy is specifically to do with mental concentration and brain work. In my case, my psychological tank runs low when working on a spreadsheet or attending a long meeting. Emotional energy is all about experiencing intense feelings and is depleted by, for example, periods of intense excitement or sadness.

But it's the last one that's the biggy. 'Relational energy', in contrast to the other three, is an energy that increases as it is exercised. This form of energy is enhanced and revitalized through positive interpersonal relationships. Cameron describes relational energy as uplifting, invigorating and rejuvenating, concluding it to be 'life-giving rather than life-depleting' (p. 51).[35]

And where does relational energy come from? People, that's where.

So, cutting to the chase, physical, psychological and emotional energy are depleted during the day. The only way to renew your energy is to mix with '2 percenters'.

The chances are you will have experienced both ends of the energy spectrum. At the lower end are the 'mood hoovers': the corporate dementors who are expert at sucking every drop of life out of you. They might be deliberate blockers and naysayers, but most mood hoovers aren't deliberately negative, they've simply learned to be a doom merchant and/or habitual moaner. Their default thinking draws them into an ultra-defensive mindset of spot-the-problem-rather-than-the-solution. However brilliant the idea, the broken record in their limited one-track juke-box is ABC's 'Shoot that poison arrow'.

A Les Brownism ...

······

'IF YOU CAN'T PICK THE PEOPLE UP IN YOUR LIFE, FOR GOODNESS SAKE DON'T LET THEM TAKE YOU DOWN.'

······

Les Brown

Of course, the mood hoovers might actually be right. Some ideas and situations are a bit shit. We get that. The problem with mood hoovers is that their default negativity kills everyone else's creativity, stone dead. What's the point of buzzing with energy, enthusiasm and ideas, if you are repeatedly shot down? Over time, it's like putting bromide in Tigger's tea. The bounce is extinguished.

Before we tackle this thorny issue, one of our counter-intuitive top tips in a book that's essentially about positivity, is to avoid the negativity witch hunt. We think a leader should create space for negativity in their teams. Managers who try to squash negativity may be inadvertently closing off channels of communication from passionate employees who are frustrated when things aren't going well. Two things to remember here. First, the naysayer might be the one brave enough to voice what everyone else is thinking and, second, they may be '2 percenters' who are experiencing dissatisfied happiness. Whatever the current state of play, they are driven to want to make things even better. They might be the ones who are agitating for change.

We are definitely *not* advocating a no-holds-barred, gung-ho cadre of unwarranted positivity. A good leader needs to hear what's not working from those who are passionate enough to care and speak up. Rather than suppress negativity, a positive leader should create a culture that allows for appropriate expression of negative feelings. By 'appropriate', we think it's about shaking your folk out of 'grumble mode', the low level of background negativity that can become a habit, and into *'what can we do about it?'* mode.

As we implied earlier, in order for your customers to be saying 'wowza' behind your back, you do have to be creative. You do have to be courageous enough to try new things, some of which won't work. So, yes, there's a place for the mood hoover's critical eye, but it needs challenging with *'OK, if you think that won't work, what do you think will work?'*

There are a whole load of better scripts – questions you can ask – that will act as a screwdriver under the rusted paint-tin of mood-hooverism. When they're grumbling about other departments, your better question might be: *I understand what you're saying. So how can we approach them to get a better working relationship?* When mood hoovers are complaining that meetings are a waste of time, your non-aggressive retort is simply: *I know what you mean. So how can we organize them better so everyone leaves with a spring in their step?*

These kinds of questions and/or statements are not a guarantee. It depends how long the rusted tin of negativity has had its lid on. And to continue the analogy to breaking point, sometimes you open up an old tin and the paint has dried up!

Mood hoover's shopping list ...

Can opener (for opening cans of worms), box of flies (to put in ointment), cat (to put amongst pigeons), bag of spanners (to put in the works)

Once more, in the interests of giving it to you straight, if it's the leader that is the mood hoover then Houston, we have a problem. Our point is that the modern workplace is tough and relentless, so leading from a position of negativity and low energy will not only harm your health and vitality, it will harm those around you.

Mental Wealth

Appraisal statement ...

'His men would follow him anywhere, but only out of morbid curiosity.'

So, the billion-dollar question (literally!) is: How can leaders create conditions that encourage staff to flourish? How can we conjure the white-heat of employee engagement?

How can we create '2 percenters'?

Once again, we're going to dare to stick our heads above the proverbial parapet and challenge conventional thinking. 'Engagement', 'mental health' and 'wellbeing' are very buzzy and a lot of very clever and well-meaning people are talking a good talk. Research undertaken by Ipsos MORI showed the importance that firms attach to wellness programmes, concluding that 'all FTSE 100 firms include wellness and engagement themes in public reporting' (p. 14).[36] However, looking behind the headline figure, the most common form of wellbeing programme is 'access to counselling' with 73 per cent of all respondents reporting that they have a counselling service available. It may well be that this is for those who are disengaged or severely stressed and, as such, is a form of wellbeing aimed at those employees who have reached their lowest ebb. If we were truly playing devil's advocate we might suggest that counselling is in place to cover their corporate backsides, avoiding litigation from those whom they've ground down to the point of being mentally unwell.

This passive approach to organizational wellbeing acts as a safety net for those in most need while failing to address the increasingly active states of satisfaction and engagement in the majority. In other words, organizational wellbeing programmes worth their salt need to maintain the motivation of those who are already flourishing *as well as* addressing the needs of those who are not.

> True (and very sad) story ...
>
> A charity fought for the release of a circus bear. Beatriz was an eight-year-old brown bear who had been trained to dance for the Russian public. She was well-travelled, secured in her 12-foot cage.
>
> After securing her release, the charity team took her to the forest and opened her cage door.
>
> Beatriz was enticed out into the vast wilderness of the Ural Mountains and spent her time pacing 12 feet by 12 feet.

Andy's research is clear. The conclusion is that '2 percenters' are satisfied, rating significantly higher than their colleagues on feelings of 'calm', 'laidback', 'relaxed' and 'at ease'. Yet they are also experiencing heightened feelings of 'enthusiasm', 'joy', 'inspiration' and 'excitement' – emotions that drive them in their pursuit of something extra. They rate significantly higher in the quadrants of 'satisfaction' AND 'engagement', as well as lower in all aspects of 'depression' and 'stress'.

For the academic nerds, 15 of these emotional differences are of statistical significance.[37]

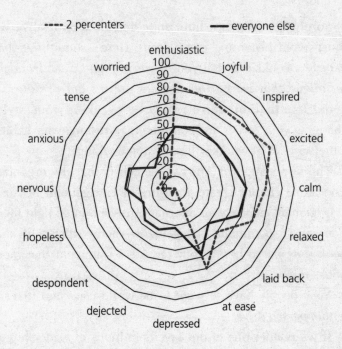

This takes a bit of getting your head around. The implication is that policies which merely aim to increase job satisfaction (i.e. give people what they want) are unlikely to create active engagement. This seems especially true when you bring in the concept of habituation. Habituation is all about the way in which things become the established norm. Motivational factors are short-lived because they become 'custom and practice' and, once embedded, lose their motivational power. It's why a pay rise only motivates in the short term. After a couple of monthly salaries, you become used to the higher level.

So engagement is a fluid state and to keep it alive we must avoid becoming complacent. Here's something that very few books ever tell you: *if you've found a motivational technique that works, the chances are it's out of date.* To avoid habituation, you have to be tweaking your style, changing your tactics and continually refreshing your habits. Otherwise, what works will soon stop working.

The implication of Andy's research is that the organization alone cannot create a culture of engagement because 'engagement' is partly an internal construct. In straight talk? You cannot command engagement. You've stuck with our book thus far so here's your reward, a statement that most books miss entirely:

Your people have to *want* to be world class and that's a *within-person drive.*

If we ponder one of our fave definitions of leadership as '*lighting fires within people rather than under them*', then intrinsic motivation describes those who have an internal pilot light and fuel supply that has fired their motivational boiler. 'Intrinsic' means motivated from within.

Straight talking once more (and it's a biggy) – true culture change is neither top-down nor bottom-up, but *inside-out.*

Flocking to Work

Building on the inside-out theme, here's a quick quiz for you; which bird is the odd one out?

Chapter 5 One for the Grown-Ups

1. Big Bird (off Sesame Street)
2. Ostrich
3. The giant teratorn of Argentina

The answer is 3, because the other two are big, but flightless. The giant teratorn (*Argentavis magnificens*) was an absolute brute of a flying bird which lived in Argentina during the late Miocene, about six million years ago. Its 30-foot wing-span meant that, whether you're a leg or breast person, the giant teratorn would have provided Christmas dinner for your entire street. However, the *Argentavis magnificens* had an unfortunate double-whammy of being ponderous and very tasty – hence its Dodoism.

Remember the shoaling mullet from earlier? The same concept applies to starlings. If you're lucky you will have marvelled at flocks of starlings, thousands of them flitting across the sky like dark clouds. It's an incredible sight as the cloud sweeps across the sky, shape-shifting as the flock changes direction.

So how is it that millions of starlings can turn together almost instantly? There are a few brave creatures flying against the flock, against conventional wisdom. As they move in another direction, they create conflict and friction, and this causes discomfort for the rest of the flock.

Organizations are often described as 'complex adaptive systems', just like a flock of starlings. 'Emergence' is the notion that the overall pattern of group behaviour emerges from individual behaviour. The emergent direction of the flock is created by the individual actions of each bird, yet the individual action of each bird is influenced by the emergent behaviour of the flock, forming a complex adaptive system.

Applied to organizations, this gives an insight of the interconnectedness of 'people' and 'culture'. Often, a culture change programme is implemented which involves forcing change through via new processes and procedures. If you've been on the receiving end of that kind of change programme, it almost certainly felt like a chore.

The emergent model suggests culture change is more viral, spreading via the changing nature of *interactions* between people. 'Culture' is nothing more than 'the way things are done around here' and, although that might encompass processes and procedures, it's really all about what's going on in the heads of your employees.

When you boil it down to its simplest component, culture is simply a set of repeating behaviours. And of course, whilst the culture affects the behaviours, the behaviours affect the culture. Just like starlings.

Following on, this means nobody is really 'in charge' of culture. Rather than being at the behest of managers, control lies in the connectedness of the people and their behaviours.

Andy's research points to happiness being a combination of genetics, circumstances and what he calls 'intentional strategies'. So hazard a guess what the biggest 'intentional strategies' are? What do you think are the two most important mental habits that '2 percenters' do and 'ordinary' people don't?

Number one, they *choose to be positive* and, two, they *make an effort to do so*. We're not going to say any more on these subjects (Andy has other books that delve into it and he's mad keen that you read them!), except to suggest that the concepts of *'consciously choosing a positive attitude'* and *'making an effort to do so'* seem simple enough.

So what's stopping you? Is it the lack of awareness that an attitudinal choice is available? Or is it simply a feeling that the effort involved in sustaining an upbeat persona is more than you have to offer?

Either way, it took Andy 12 years of hard study to find out things that starlings already know! Flocking behaviour requires a few brave souls to go first and, when you reach a critical mass, the rest will follow.

Chapter 6
LISTENING FOR DUMMIES

• • • • • •

Starting with a quiz (in which we're guaranteeing you will shine) and finishing with a story of a football manager and a box of oranges, in-between we deal in drugs as well as hard and soft skills, sinking you into a quagmire with the concept that the soft ones are hard and the hard ones easy.

We cover the basics of listening and praise, suggesting that the classic 'feedback sarnie' has not just curled up at the edges, but has been around so long it's gone rancid.

It is our belief that you can learn from trauma, so we share our winner of 'worst delegate to have ever attended a leadership programme' before flipping into the more productive world of 'how to win friends and influence people' which shows that the world might have changed, but the basic principles of human connection are as steadfast as ever.

Eyes down, quiz time. No cheating now …

How *Not* to Do It

Oh my gosh, another quiz! Calm yourself and then gauge whether you're above or below average for these activities:

- Driving
- Happiness
- Honesty

Evidence suggests most people rate themselves as well above average in them all. My knowledge of stats isn't great but I understand the concept of 'average' and I know we can't all be above the bar. This points to something called 'illusory superiority' or the 'above average effect', and listening is a crucial leadership skill that suffers with the same problem.

So please don't be tempted to skip this chapter with a throw-away *I don't need to read this bit because I'm a great listener.* While that statement *might* be true, there's a very strong likelihood you're suffering from a positive illusion.[38]

Before we get to grips with the basics of what's right, it might be worth pointing out how to get it badly wrong. In one of Andy's first ever workshops he encountered a senior manager who, for anonymity's sake, we'll call 'Steve' (he was actually called Roy). Little did Andy know that Roy would go down in the annals of history as 'worst delegate ever'. Here's the headline news.

Andy did what all decent trainers do, he settled the room and announced, *'Welcome to what we boldly call 'The Art of*

Being Brilliant'. It's a day of happiness and positivity. A day like no other. A day that might even change your life.' Yes, he does get a little over-excited. *'But before we kick-off,'* he smiled, *'does anyone have any questions?'*

One hand raised, noticeable in its weariness. Andy looked at the delegate's name card. *'Yes Roy,'* he beamed. *'What's your question?'*

Roy fixed Andy with an icy stare and growled, *'What the hell can you teach me?'*

Andy was about to squeak some sort of answer but didn't have chance. Roy was just getting started. *'Do I look happy?'* he asked, rhetorically. *'If I go back to work happy, they'll think I'm on something. And do you know what?'* he said, *'I've worked here 29 years and I haven't had a good day yet.'*

Andy's mouth opened and closed silently, words failing to come out.

'I've got a calendar on my desk and every day I tick off another day because it's another day closer to retirement. And anyway,' snarled our senior manager, now in reflective mood, *'this positive stuff will never work, because my team's demoralized.'*

There was a collective group sigh. The other delegates had suffered Roy forever. Let me remind you, he was a senior manager, his crushing style famous for short bursts of action before good people sussed him out and left the organization. Roy's admission that *'I take young enthusiastic people into my team and knock it out of them early on'* was bad enough, the fact he said it with pride was beyond the pale. It's true,

Roy's team was demoralized, because Roy was the chief demoralizer; his aggression and negativity kicked the shit out of any initiative, ideas or enthusiasm.

> Comment on an appraisal form
>
> *He's not got ulcers, but he's a carrier.*

The reason Roy sticks in my head is not merely because his leadership style is exactly the opposite of what's required in the modern workplace, but because I'm reminded of him every day I log on to my computer. Above my desk is a framed 'happy sheet' (the end of course feedback where delegates get to rate their experience) and, in answer to the question *What have you learned today?*, one of the delegates wrote, *'I'm not going to end up like Roy'.*

That's the best learning ever! The painful thing about that story is not just that it's true, and that countless good people have had their enthusiasm ripped from their lives by an awful manager, but it's also an aching realization for Roy – he isn't going to get another go at those 29 years. They're done and dusted. A third of his life, what could and should have been his best years, have dragged by in a torpor of misery.

You are not Roy. Roy would never read a book about leadership and, if by some miracle this book fell into his hands, he would hate it because it goes against everything he knows. But Roy is real. The story is extreme, but versions of

Roy exist. Toxic managers who create a stifling atmosphere. If we give Roy the benefit of the doubt, we might be able to make an argument that his style suited, once, back in the industrial revolution, where employees didn't need to think. But the times when managers 'managed' and workers 'worked' are dead and buried. That means old ways of leading are ashes to ashes and the central role, which you always thought was to motivate your people, is dust to dust.

Sign of the times?

A sign seen on a manager's door: *Ignore me as appropriate to get your job done.*

When Hard is Easy and Soft is Hard

There's a lot of talk about 'hard' and 'soft' leadership skills, and we think they're wrongly named. So-called 'hard' skills tend to be things you've learned at school – the ability to manipulate a spreadsheet, write an adequate press release or use PowerPoint, for example. Soft skills are more subtle – things like the ability to listen, ask the right questions, motivate, inspire, empathize, create trust and get on someone's wavelength.

We think, on balance, the hard skills are easy, at least in respect of 'you can go on a course and learn about spreadsheets', whereas soft skills are rock hard. Sometimes derided as 'pink and fluffy', the skill set that enables you to inspire people to go above their job description cannot be learned in college or even from a book. Sure, we can provide some clues, but soft skills involve emotions, and no book in the world can teach you the exact science of how to manage your own emotions, never mind the emotions of others.

So herein lies another raft of very simple principles, the ground rules, stuff that almost goes without saying, but that we'll say anyway. Things like listening, giving credit to those who deserve it, sometimes even handing over some of your credit to them. Sticking up for people and saying nice things about your colleagues behind their back. Apologizing when you get things wrong, being respectful of their family time, putting training into areas in which they're already strong, asking for their ideas ...

It's a never-ending list so we'll cherry pick. Listening might not solve all your leadership worries, but it's probably the single most important thing anyone can do to make a real connection with their team – so here's our guide to the hardest soft skill of them all ...

Rewind. That previous sentence is badly written. Not the 'hardest soft' bit (that's clever!), but the 'skill' bit. Listening is often described as a skill. It is, partly. But it's also a *choice*.

When you are communicating with someone, the key question is: where is the focus of your attention – is it upon you, or is it upon them?

'*Watching their lips move waiting for your turn to speak*' is not listening any more than '*having an analytical *conversation in your head about how their viewpoint differs from yours'* is not listening. Ditto *'drifting off thinking about what you're having for tea tonight'*, *'furtively scanning your emails'* or *'responding to them while pretending to make notes'*.

All of the above are very easy to do, hence why listening is a lot harder than it seems. The key is to be focussed on *them*, and your primary goal is to seek to understand *their* perspective rather than sharing yours. Remember we talked about the value of diversity in the team earlier? Value that they have a different perspective, be curious about it, be fascinated by how they have come up with a differing viewpoint from you. And when you do that your connection with them will flourish.

The minimum ratio you should be aiming for on the first indicator is 2:1; you have two ears and one mouth for a reason. But if you really want to be a great listener some suggest you aim for 10:1 (list-*ten*). Whatever you go for, our recommendation is listen more than talk and always be aware of the ratio.

The next indicator may be a bit of a shocker. Start taking notice of the number of times you interrupt the person you are with. We're pretty sure you'll be surprised at how often you do it. Now STOP IT! The bottom line with interruptions is whatever your intention is, the reality is you are squashing their input and they really feel it when you do it. There are certain circumstances where you will need to interrupt and it is a useful tool, but these will be rare so only do it wilfully and with care.

Now for the third indicator. When you speak you could be sharing your opinion, relaying facts, suggesting a particular course of action or perhaps disagreeing with someone. These are all necessary in a good discussion – and they are all about you. When we have observed meetings using this idea then often 80–90 per cent of what comes out of people's mouths is a combination of interruptions and *'me and my ideas'* (called 'advocacy').

'Them and their ideas' (called 'inquiry') involves asking questions (real questions that is, not statements with a question mark at the end), supporting and building on other people's ideas, checking you understand what someone has said, summarizing where the discussion has got to so far. It can also be about bringing other people and opinions into the conversation, particularly when there are two differing views or there are strong voices monopolizing the debate. All of these demonstrate that your focus is on others and will build connection and buy-in from the team.

Adding a dash of science to it, Marcial Losada and Emily Heaphy[39] observed managers and their teams concluding that, typically, teams had a 2:1 positivity ratio; with high performing teams registering 6:1 and low performing teams slashing each other in a corporate bloodbath of 1:1. This corresponds with John Gottman's (1994) work on relationships, in which flourishing marriages have a positivity ratio of 5:1 and failed marriages 1:1.[40] The slasher movie can happen with family communication too. Just saying!

Top Tip

Here's our reminder for when you're in charge of a meeting: your job is not to select the best ideas, it is to create a great environment that allows the very best ideas to emerge.

Advanced Listening

Ninja level

You need to understand that 'listen' is an anagram of 'silent'.

Most managers are very good at finding solutions to problems. Sometimes the hardest part of being a leader is finding the right question. What is the problem we're trying to solve? There's a really interesting corporate tale which may well be folklore but it's worth telling anyway. Many years ago, as myth and legend have it, a cosmetics manufacturer (of hair and beauty fame) invited all their movers and shakers to a huge conference in an exotic country. Their aim was to come up with a snazzy new marketing campaign and a strapline for a perplexing problem: their products were a little bit more expensive than their competitors, so why on earth should customers pay extra for a product when they could get exactly the same for less?

Three days later, the great and the good had brainstormed, thought outside the box and done some blue sky thinking until the clouds rolled in. And still no magic solution. The conference came to an end and the 300 highly trained corporate beasts threw back their coiffured locks and traipsed out of the resort, their creativity battered and beaten.

The woman on reception saw that they were downbeat and asked one of the delegates what was wrong. *'We've just spent three days trying to come up with a marketing campaign that will persuade our customers to spend extra on our products. I mean, why should you?'*

Apparently, the receptionist shrugged and offered, *'Because you're worth it?'*

A slogan was born and a global campaign launched. The moral of the story is that sometimes the best solutions come from the most unlikely places, so it's imperative that you get everyone involved – and listen!

As a leader, you should lean away from *'Here's the problem and this is what I'm proposing we do about it'* and towards *'Here's the challenge – any ideas?'* This simple shift of emphasis is much more likely to get buy-in from your team. This is B+ listening, it's likely to generate novel ideas and creative solutions but, in school report terms, you 'can do better'.

A* listening is very advanced indeed. It's super simple and will send your 'connection-ometer' off the scale, but it takes some guts so you may want to build a while at B+

before going for it. You're already letting them share in creating the solution, but this time ask them: *What do you think the problem is?*

This is difficult because it goes against the grain. Leaders often feel the need to have all the answers, so asking questions can feel like you're shirking your leadership responsibility. We promise you, asking great questions is your modern-day leadership responsibility. This is about you valuing your team members and the diversity of thought they bring to the point where you believe that there may be a better perspective on what the problem is than yours, or that other viewpoints will help shape the problem statement better. You can run your meetings any way you want, but we think that A* listening is the best way to engage your team.

In today's hurly burliness, there's a luxury item that you need to save up for if you want to keep getting A* in listening. Luxury because it takes time and focus; guaranteed A* because it will forge strong connections. We'll call it 'quiet listening' because you bin all those mental distractions and just focus on the person you are with. Just them and you, with you totally focussed on them – it's powerful.

Dale Carnegie's all-time classic rule of how to win friends and influence people is to be interested in them.[41] *Genuinely* interested. Have you ever heard anything so simple, and yet so effective? It's spooky how the science of human interaction works but trust us – when you choose to be interested in others you become much more interesting.

The thing with listening is it takes time. Time most of us don't have because of the busyness, and when we assess it, at that moment, the easy choice is to trade listening for the time saved. We reckon that pound for pound, choosing listening over saving time is probably the leadership equivalent of 'buy one and get ten free'. It's the best deal you can ever do. A leadership no-brainer. The person speaking already knows how important your time is. When you're investing that time in them they feel valued, motivated and engaged and their feeling of self-worth increases. When you're listening you will understand them at a much deeper level and you will understand what's going on with the speaker. It won't be just about the words, your emotional intelligence spider sense will connect with how they are feeling.

Yes there will be times as a leader when you have to lay down the law, when you need to give clear direction and control the agenda. Being a brilliant leader isn't just about sitting back with your feet on the desk having deep and meaningful discussions with your staff whilst stroking your chin wisely. But it's not about being the superhero with all the answers either. Remember from earlier, the most powerful thing you can do is to NOT offer solutions, but instead support your team in shaping their own and giving them the space to deliver. Quiet listening is a gift. It can only be given and, when it is, your team will flourish.

Drug Dealing

A famous footballer tells a leadership story in his autobiography. Keeping names out of it, England kicked off a World Cup campaign with a disappointing draw against a lowly ranked nation. After the game, the players sat, shoulders slumped and eyes on their boots, as the manager laid into them. Every player was getting a dressing down, their performance ripped to shreds by a manager who was under massive pressure. Until the team captain raised his head, looked directly at the ranting manager, and said, *'Boss, have you ever considered, the problem might be you?'*

In football-speak they call it 'losing the dressing room'. That manager didn't last much longer.

Let's provide another cold flannel that acts as a slap round the face to remind you of something you already know: praise is one of the most powerful motivators in existence – so much so that being praised triggers the release of dopamine, a chemical in our brains that helps control feelings of reward and pleasure. As well as making us feel great, dopamine can also enable more innovative thinking and creative problem-solving at work. Yes, it's a chemical that makes you feel great and it's legal and free but be careful, it's the same chemical reaction when drinking and taking drugs.

The research on this topic is everywhere – feel free to Google at your leisure, or simply think back to how you felt when you last received genuine recognition or praise for a job well done. And the great thing about appreciation is that it doesn't just feel great to receive it – if you reflect on your own experience of giving genuine appreciation you will know it also feels great to give it. When it comes to feedback, what's not to like?

The great Zig Ziglar used to quip that motivation was like bathing. Both wear off, hence you need to do them daily. Genuine appreciation, heartfelt praise, catching people doing things well and telling them – commit them to your daily routine. Otherwise, things can get stinky.

Here are a few simple things to consider. It doesn't have to be in public with fanfares and waves of applause – in fact some of your team members would hate you if this was your approach to praise! In most instances, it is simply a conversation where you:

- Make sure it's a good time to speak to them.
- Talk specifically about what they did.
- Explain how you felt as a result.
- Thank them.
- Reflect afterwards on their response.

For example, '*I thought the way you handled that customer was fantastic. You listened, came up with a solution and turned them around. It makes me proud to see customers handled so well. Thank you. It reflects well on the whole team.*'

Timing is key because if their attention is embroiled in something else and they haven't got time for the conversation then it will have little impact. Don't waste good praise by letting it get lost in the noise.

You may also want to apply the 'feed-forward' principle in which you add a suggestion for the future, for example: *'in the future, if you applied this resourcefulness to other customers, I'm sure we'll all feel the benefit'.*

To ensure you get it right, get your intention right. Praise should be given with the intent to motivate and encourage, not to manipulate or exploit. It's about gratitude, not platitude and the receiver will be able to tell the difference. Make sure your praise is Timely, Often, Sincere and Specific. We thought very briefly about trademarking this but TOSS™ could be a challenge to market. *Moving on ...*

We threw in 'Timely' there as it's really important to give praise promptly. Yes, we've all got to do annual appraisals, but if you'd just done a stormingly good job on something, how would you feel if the boss patted you on the back and said that they'll discuss it in 11 months' time? You'd want to know what you'd done well, how it had made them feel and that they meant every word of it.

Of course, tying in with our oxymoron of 'soft skills are rock hard', it is essential that we get to know our teams as individuals because, when it comes to praise and recognition, different things work for different people – that's why it's useful to reflect on their response and consider what you could do differently next time.

In the busy lives we lead, it is almost certain that you are not giving enough appreciation – not just at work but also at home. And if you are reading this thinking that you would love to *receive* more appreciation yourself, take our word for it – appreciation sets off ripples around us. The more we give out, the more we receive back (eventually!). In a bizarre world of reciprocity, if you would like to start receiving more appreciation – start giving it.

The Difficult Stuff

······

'ANYONE CAN START SOMETHING NEW. IT TAKES REAL LEADERS TO STOP SOMETHING OLD.'

······

Dan Rockwell

Positive feedback is incredibly powerful, and yet it's only part of the equation, because leadership also involves talking about the difficult stuff too. Some people are easy to praise, because they're constantly brilliant. But not everybody's praiseworthy, right?

Michael Bungay Stanier talks about the seven dysfunctional dwarves: Sulky, Moany, Shouty, Crabby, Martyr-y, Touchy and Petulant.[42] (*I would like to add an extra one into the mix: Can't-be-arsed-y.*) I used to share an office with them all! In fact, I think I might have been one of them (I was Martyr-y; '*look at me working really hard while you lot all grumble and gripe*').

112

Now to the hard bit. You've done everything you could possibly do and created a brilliant environment. Most of the team are loving it, but some still aren't engaged. This is the bit that gets swept under the carpet in this type of book so we thought we'd confront it head on. As the language of love says, you cannot force someone to love you or, if you prefer an old classic, you can't polish a turd.

The best leaders deal with difficult conversations promptly because they know that leaving underperformers to underperform sends a more powerful message than anything they say. Jose Mourinho tells a snappy anecdote along the lines of *'if you have one bad orange in a box, very soon all the oranges will be bad'*.

The format for negative or re-directive feedback is the same as positive feedback, but in this case the feed-forward aspect becomes essential to correct the behaviour: *How could you do it better next time?*

And, of course, who can forget the staple diet of management courses from the 1980s onwards, the classic 'feedback sandwich'. The aim was to slip bad news in-between two positives: *You keep your desk tidy. Your work is shit. Ooh, nice shoes.* This is piss poor advice so we'd be really grateful if you would expunge it from your repertoire. In fact we insist, as it just confuses things. It's better to get straight to the point: *'I need to tell you something you're not going to like. Let's sit down.'* Then deliver the message in the standard format.

So if you have some difficult conversations outstanding, that have been residing on your 'to-do' list for too long, or you've just been actively ignoring them; we challenge you to get a list together and get them done. If you need to get advice first, do it quickly and then get them done. Let's set a target. All done by the end of next week. Excellent!

Why not balance that off by making a more positive list:

- Column 1 – all the members of your team, key colleagues, the boss and everyone who is important to you outside of work.
- Column 2 – against each name put something you genuinely appreciate that they did this week.

Once you've done that go and give them the wonderful feedback. Once you've done that put a slot in your diary every week to do the same.

Repeat. Repeat. Repeat. Keep repeating.

Make sure you are giving out significantly more positive feedback than negative. This, of course, involves spending more time catching people doing things right than catching them doing things wrong. Implement this at home too. Recalling the communication ratios from earlier, if you can register six positives for every negative (remember it's not 6 to none – this is not *The Waltons*, you are allowed some negativity), you will be breathing life into your team.

The added bonus is that you will create the kind of environment in which difficult conversations become fewer and won't end up being that difficult.

Chapter 7

THE LEADERSHIP LOVE MACHINE

· · · · · ·

Starting with hot stuff and ending with lashings of love, this chapter is our '50 shades', a simmering cauldron of steamy leadership passion.

We prove why it's impossible NOT to communicate (even when you say nothing) and, in a roundabout way, hint at why you're so crucial with The Clash song, 'Should I Stay or Should I Go?'

We revisit corporate rules and advocate that you let go of the control joystick, mentioning pigeon shit along the way. We stifle a yawn at the GROW model (I know, how totally maverick of us!) before introducing Mabel, the creative genius that nobody ever listens to. We end up treating you to our 'cheat codes' (everything you need to know about coaching, squeezed into a couple of pages).

We challenge you to get lazy which, because of the kind of person you are, will rile you at first blush but, on reflection, we think you'll go with it.

Finishing with a love-in. Leadership porn! Nice!

Hot stuff

Empathy is a hot topic. Well, if not scalding, at least it's simmering steadily. A brief trawl through recent psychological history suggests that Freud had us by the short and curlies what with his theories about repressed feelings and sexual desires. It's bizarre that a man who came up with the 'anal stage' of childhood development (basically, that your potty training determines your character) has held such sway over the psychological world for so long. You can Google his 'oral' and 'phallic' stages of development for yourself.

Of course, Freud's point is that deep down in the primitive part of our brain, we are driven purely by repressed sexual desires. Thankfully, our brains have moved with the times. The bit at the front of your brain, behind your eyebrows, is a fairly recent manifestation and this so-called pre-frontal cortex is what differentiates us from other animals. This part of your brain not only serves the useful purpose of keeping your hat on, it also provides evidence of our transformation into 'homo empathicus' – that we are actually wired for societal interest.

How it works ...

People don't care what you know until they know that you care.

Empathy is second nature to most humans, so much so that people lacking it are regarded as dangerous, psychotic or mentally ill. It extends the boundaries of the self well beyond our physical skin and bones. Empathy allows humans to be in a perpetual state of communication: reading people, intuiting, stepping into their minds, assuming and sensing. Indeed, you cannot *NOT* communicate.

If you think about it, empathy has to be built into our brains, otherwise society would fall apart? Mothers would ignore the crying of their new-borns, charities would be skint and your friends would yawn with tedium as you regaled them with the story of your unfaithful partner. There would be no point in going to watch a horror film, a comedy or a football match and the internet would be devoid of videos of pets being cute. Just like a fish has never figured out it's in water, empathy is all around us to the point we're so immersed, we take it for granted.

The self-interest story goes back a very long way. In the 1600s, Thomas Hobbes argued that if left to their own devices, humanity would come crashing down in a 'war of all against all'.[43] Hobbes reckoned we are so inherently violent and self-interested that the only thing that could save us was government setting laws to keep us in check.

If we relate this to how organizations are designed, ask yourself what protocols, job descriptions, person specs, procedures, policies, regulations and car park permits are actually for? The answer is three things: control, control and control!

Organizations inadvertently end up stifling creativity and awesomeness. One person can't be trusted to turn up to work on time so rather than sort that person out, the managers devise a clocking-in system, so *everyone* has to provide evidence of their whereabouts. One person once got bored at work and spent an hour on Facebook, so now *everyone* gets a warning about social media. One person skives off work with 'a bad back' and spends their day at Alton Towers so now *everyone* has to have back-to-work interviews (tell me when you're bored ...) One person leaves a dirty plate in the sink and now there's a sign in the kitchen, in bold SHOUTY letters that *EVERYONE* MUST WASH UP AND PUT THEIR CUPS AND PLATES AWAY. One person once wrote an inappropriate email and now *everyone* has to have a three-paragraph disclaimer on their email signature.

Genuine email signature received today (the organization anonymized to protect you from wanting to firebomb them):

The Council welcomes correspondence in English and Welsh and we will ensure that we communicate with you in the language of your choice, whether that's English, Welsh or bilingual as long as you let us know which you prefer. Corresponding in Welsh will not lead to any delay. Privileged/Confidential Information may be contained in this message. If you are not the addressee indicated in this message (or responsible for delivery of the message to such person), you may not copy or deliver this message to anyone. In such case, you should destroy this message and kindly notify the sender by reply email. Please advise immediately if you or your employer does not consent to Internet email for messages of this kind. Opinions, conclusions and other information in this message that do not relate to the official business of the Council of the City and County of xxxx shall be understood as neither given nor endorsed by it. All e-mail sent to or from this address will be processed by xxxx County Council's Corporate E-mail system and may be subject to scrutiny by someone other than the addressee.

The result is that too many organizations are haemorrhaging brilliant people. The incompatibility of the strangulating control of corporate life is most keenly felt by the uber-talented, where they are stifled, frustrated and contained. The rules you see, they've been put in place to corral the idiots, but they also clip the wings of those willing and able to soar. After a couple of years hopping around ankle deep in bird shit, they've had enough. They can fly, so they do.

McKinsey's 'War for talent' survey[44] suggested 58 per cent of employees say they work for an underperforming manager and, of those, 86 per cent said it made them want to leave.

The stats also work the other way – working for a good manager means you want to stay. This is a powerful bottom-line message; you can have the best strategy in the world, the most exciting website, gym membership and flexitime, but if your immediate manager is rubbish, then you're screwed!

You will never achieve 'world class' through control. The only way to create an environment where everyone feels compelled to give their best is to create an environment of trust. But, of course, that would mean letting go of the control joystick and that requires courage. Someone's going to mess up, guaranteed! (Which is why 'control' was put there in the first place, remember?)

The Cheat Code

Stress reduction top tip …

Esquire magazine's editor, 'AJ' Jacobs, was so busy that he needed a personal assistant. He offloaded all the mundane stuff to start with and, once they'd mastered that, his PA graduated to manage some assignments he didn't fancy. One day, in a flash of enlightenment, AJ realized he was worrying about a big project he was working on so he decided to outsource the worry.

Let me be clear, he didn't hand over the project, just the fretting. He asked his assistant if she would worry about the project for him, thereby releasing him extra time to focus on it in a positive way. She agreed. And every day when he started to ruminate he'd remind himself that his PA was already on the case and he'd relax.[45]

I've heard the key to coaching lies in three principles: being lazy, curious and often.

Laziness is one of those words that immediately stands out, probably in an irritating way? You never get a minute to yourself, so 'laziness' is definitely something you're not and not something you intend to become, right? You're overwhelmed, you've got too much on, you've got emails that date back to 2011 that you haven't answered yet. No matter how up-to-date you are on the latest productivity hack, no matter which app you've recently downloaded for your gadget, you're never going to get on top of this stuff. If I asked your team, guess what? *Ditto!*

We are trying to pull together the best of what we know to produce the most awesome all-round leadership book on the planet, and so when it comes to 'coaching' what are we supposed to do? There are whole tomes written on coaching, from your classic GROW model to your quick and dirty *Coaching for Dummies*.

My teenage son lives in PlayStation land and he once got stuck on a level so bought some 'cheat codes': quick wins that allowed him to power ahead. So, here are your coaching cheat codes, the absolute highlights, scrunching this very powerful leadership 'style' into half a chapter.

It's fair to say that most leaders 'get' the point of coaching. It combines all the stuff we've been talking about. You already know that coaching is about spending time with your folks and chatting, listening, praising, empathy ... *blah blah blah* ... with the aim of inspiring and empowering them to go make a dent in the universe.

And yet most leaders don't do nearly enough of it. There are two primary reasons: firstly, you've been on a course but you're still a bit uncomfortable with the whole thing, and secondly (the real reason) – *who on earth's got time to sit around having one-to-ones when there's so much on your to-do list?* Coaching is the Harrods of leadership styles. It's a leadership aisle we like to browse, we pick it up, examine it, but its price tag is unaffordable.

Looking at excuse number one. The reason you're uncomfortable with coaching is that it's surprisingly difficult to change old habits. As Michael Bungay Stanier suggests, 'Giving a little less advice and asking a few killer questions' is counter-intuitive. You end up rationalizing: '*I've spent my entire corporate life giving advice and getting promoted for it, so knowing the answers and volunteering them has pretty much got me to where I am*'. Coaching, somewhat uncomfortably, turns all that on its head. If I have to *ask questions* doesn't that imply I don't know the answers? And all that *listening* – that really slows up the conversation.

Well, the short answers are 'no' and 'yes'. Stanier talks of an overdependency culture – a workplace where you've accidentally trained your people to be totally reliant on you. This is disempowering for them and deeply frustrating for you. You have (albeit totally innocently) worked so hard at creating over-dependency that you are stupidly busy and *you* are the bottleneck in the system. Your team is paralysed while they await your decision.

This is just one of the reasons why you have to bite the bullet and instil a coaching habit – it releases you and them! Basically, there's being 'helpful' as in growing your people and 'helpful' as in stepping in and taking over. Once you're locked into the latter your good intentions backfire in an over-dependency culture. Why would your staff ever learn to do anything for themselves if they can call you and you'll sort it?

Efficiency. A modern parable …

I once knew an employee who took great pride in how efficiently he managed his department. He worked in an office with a flat roof and one day during some heavy rain one of his staff, Joe, brought to his attention the fact that the roof was leaking and water was dripping into the office. This efficient manager immediately went and found a metal wastepaper basket and placed it under the drips. Sorted!

About an hour later, Joe came and told him the bucket was nearly full. Our manager soon found another, placed that under the drip, emptied the first and placed it alongside ready to be filled again. Now a simple system was in place.

Our manager felt very pleased with his efficiency. '*But wait*', he thought. '*Why, as a manager, do I not delegate the bucket emptying to Joe? This will surely be a case of job enrichment, added responsibility and employee development?*' During the next storm, he therefore coached Joe in the process and skills required and handed over the responsibility to him. Genius!

He, of course, monitored Joe's performance on a regular basis. Alas, as often happens in these situations, Joe soon left the organization. However, the manager saw this as a golden opportunity. Why not include responsibility for bucket emptying in the job description? So when Martha started work in Joe's old job, she took on the additional responsibility, with training of course.

This was now seen as the height of efficient management. Only one last possibility remained to be explored – and yes, there was a device available which could be placed on the roof of the office to tell the computer when it was raining. The computer would then send a message to Martha's desk, reminding her to empty the bucket. Perfect!

Now our efficient manager has a fool-proof process ensuring the drip was dealt with. He was, of course, promoted for demonstrating such efficiency. His replacement is currently working with the team on the design of an automated bucket emptying device.

Meanwhile Mabel, who cleans the office, keeps asking: *'Why doesn't someone mend the fucking roof!'*

Cool Coaching Questions

As well as a certain skill set, coaching does require a chunk of time (and a determination to do it).

There's a whole raft of interesting coaching questions. Some of our faves are:

- What is it that made you take the time to see me?
- What are the issues? And what might lie behind them?
- What's the real problem you are trying to solve?
- What's the best you could hope for?
- What would happen if you do nothing?
- What might be a good starting point for you?
- What might some quick wins be for you?
- What would you like to do next?
- What's the best question I could ask you next?

Or, perhaps the most powerful subconscious question in the world:

- If you did know the answer, what would it be?'

Most coaches swear by Sir John Whitmore's GROW model.[46] He's a Sir for a reason, right? Sitting down and coaching your team through:

- What are your Goals?
- What's the Reality? (i.e., where are you now?)
- What Options do you have?
- What's the Will to move forward?

Apart from the 'W' not really fitting the acronym, the real problem is that GROW is feeling just a little bit jaded. We prefer the snazzy, slightly quirky approach of Michael Bungay Stanier.[47] His coaching questions are:

- Kickstart question: *What's on your mind?*
- AWE question: *And what else?*
- Focus question: *What's the real challenge here for you?*
- Foundation question: *What do you want?*
- Lazy question: *How can I help?*
- Strategic question: *If you're saying yes to this, what are you saying no to?*
- Learning question: *What was most useful for you?*

No messing folks. Loads of conscious and subconscious stuff. Cherry pick the questions to suit the situation and then shut up, while your coachee frames the problem and solves it for themselves.

Of course, coaching is just one of your available styles. Daniel Goleman[48] suggests that the most emotionally intelligent leader will choose a style, as one would a golf club. In the same way you wouldn't tee off with a putter (wrong club for the job), if someone pops their head round your door and asks *'Have you seen Brenda?'*, you wouldn't go into coaching mode and say, *'Grab a seat. It's not really about Brenda is it. Tell me, what's the real challenge here for you?'* Someone will punch you. Very hard. Deservedly!

Coaching has its place and herein lies the difficulty. It's another of those rock hard soft skills that's only effective if used in the right amount. Overuse it and your staff will roll their eyes. Underuse it and they'll feel unloved. It ties in with Maslow's basic needs of safety and love.[49]

Evan Gordon talks about the 'fundamental organizing principle of the brain', in which it scans the environment five times a second, looking for danger.[50] If it's safe, your brain relaxes and is able to operate at its most sophisticated and creative level. You assume positive intent of the people around you and tap into collective wisdom. Barbara Fredrickson[51] calls it 'broaden and build', where your brain lights up and can see opportunities and solutions. This is where you need the brains of your team to be.

If your brain sniffs danger or threat, it closes down. Resources are diverted to fight or flight. Note, this isn't 'danger' as in 'there's a tiger loose in the building': your brain will trip into emergency mode when it's overwhelmed with busyness, there's another restructure looming or you have to do a presentation to the board. Cue lack of creativity, less engagement with the people around you and a sense of distrust and mild panic (aka *'how most people feel most of the time'*).

> ### Latin Lesson
>
> *Semper in merda; sola altitudo variat*
>
> **Translation:** We're always in the shit; it's just the depth that varies

Coaching is so powerful because, if done correctly, it creates a feeling of safety and love. Yes, we said love. Now, personally, my head is immediately ringing with warning claxons signifying dangerous levels of pinkness and fluff. Geoff Aigner weighs in with his suggestion that leading is about growth: '... and things grow with love'. The claxons get louder as Aigner digs in deeper with: 'Love helps us remember our purpose and who we are really serving.'[52]

Thankfully, Aigner acknowledges the ringing in my head, noting that it's not just me; we all have a problem with talking about love at work and love in leadership. Barbara Fredrickson calms me by suggesting we set aside our pre-conceived narrow view and to think of love as being 'an interpersonally situated and socially shared experience of one or more positive emotions'.[53]

And, phew, the sirens go quiet. In its broadest sense, leading requires us to go beyond concern for ourselves to have concern and care for others. We need love to support us when we take risks, to grow, to protect us from becoming cynical, anxious, and scared, to keep us steady. Coaching is perhaps the most powerful way of telling your people that you care. The tacit message is that I value you, I trust you, you're worth listening to and I want to help make you even more awesome than you currently are.

And I can't help thinking the previous paragraph sounds rather like 'love'.

Chapter 8

MIND THE GAP

● ● ● ● ● ● ●

What have Eliza Doolittle and a Golem got in common? Erm, nothing really. They're opposites, and that's our starting point in a chapter that goes from piss-takers to 'positive deviance' and our very first official-looking 'theory in a box' – you know, the kind of thing that you'd expect in a 'normal' leadership book?

We look at why organizations are fixated on problem solving to the point that some people have become black belts!

We advocate the opposite, a culture of trust and abundance, and give a couple of quick wins that will help you on your way.

We have a sneaky suspicion that this chapter is a lot cleverer than it looks?

Pygmalion or Golem?

······

'THE GREATEST MISTAKE YOU CAN MAKE IN LIFE IS TO CONTINUALLY BE AFRAID YOU WILL MAKE ONE.'

······

Elbert Hubbard

You may well have heard of the 'Pygmalion effect': the phenomenon whereby folk live up to assumptions made about them. It's captured really well in the classic folklore classroom example where a new maths teacher was told she had the top set and six months later they had achieved top set grades. It was only then that it became apparent there had been a mix-up and the kids she'd been teaching were actually bottom set. Her high expectations had altered both her and the children's reality and they smashed it!

The opposite is the 'Golem effect', encapsulated in the classic mood hoover appraisal statement of *sets low standards and continually fails to achieve them.* In 'little-l' speak, if you assume and treat your employees like they are untrustworthy and work-shy, who only come to work to do the minimum they can get away with for the maximum return, guess what? They'll behave exactly like that. Douglas McGregor calls them Theory X managers: they have low expectations, trust nobody and end up being a little bit control-freaky.[54]

Theory Y managers hold the opposite assumptions. They assume all staff are hardworking, trustworthy, able to take responsibility, motivated by achievement and recognition and the source of fabulous ideas. As you'd expect – the chances are they will be.

The Pygmalion effect is such a powerful notion, so let's think about it from the employee's perspective for a moment. Recall the worst manager you have ever had – the one who did your thinking for you because, of course, they assumed you weren't capable. They weren't big on praise because they assumed you were motivated by your end of month pay cheque. They never bothered asking your opinion because you weren't capable of having an original thought. Ask yourself, did that manager bring out the best in you, or were you getting home exhausted, frustrated and scanning the 'jobs vacant' websites?

What about your 'hero" manager who looked for the best in you? We're hoping you have had a manager who believed in you, trusted you, listened to your ideas and acted upon them. How hard did you work for that particular manager?

The fact that our belief in another person's potential brings that potential to life, shows up time and time again. Why not take the advice of Richard Branson who says that organizations should simply 'Hire good people and then get the hell out of their way'. Once again, its delicious simplicity is the reason we love it. You hired that particular person because of who they are and what you saw, so stop trying to iron them out to conform to some sort of corporate stereotype.

Top Tip

Our Pygmalion top tip is to start assuming your people are capable of great things and want to do a great job. Then watch them deliver.

You may now be shouting at this book: *But you've never had someone like [insert name of your most difficult staff member here] working for you!* We're not so dumb as to think it will work for everyone, but it will work for most people, most of the time.

We think that we all learn as much from those dreadful managers we have worked for, as we do from those we would class as our 'heroes', so here's a little exercise for you. Fill in the grid below with the worst and best managers you've ever had.

Worst manager ever	What did they do?	How did I feel?

Best manager ever	What did they do?	How did I feel?

Now compare and contrast. What's the learning? It'll be something along the lines of: *under poor leaders we feel like we work for the company, whereas under good leaders we feel like we work for each other.* The world class boss listened, trusted and smiled. They probably had more faith in you than you had in yourself with amazing results – you grew! Work was a joy.

The opposite was, well, *the opposite*. Work felt like work.

You don't have to be a sport nut to have heard of the All Blacks: the most formidable international rugby team on the planet – from New Zealand, population *not quite 5 million*. How the heck does NZ manage to conquer the rugby world? Lots of reasons, but one that stands out is their recruitment policy which comprises all of two words: '*No Dickheads*'.

Try sticking that in your next recruitment advert!

In *Legacy*, James Kerr says it unequivocally – there are many world class players who have never pulled on the All Black jersey.[55] They might be loaded with talent. They might even have more talent than the players wearing the actual jersey, but they're not the right fit. Their 'no dickheads' policy means life inside the camp is a whole lot easier.

You might have accidentally admitted a few into your organization so we need you to go further than the All

Blacks. 'No Dickheads' might stop any more coming in, but you might also need a policy of 'Get Rid of the Existing Dickheads'.

Yes, we know. The language might be obtuse (which is why we love it) but the meaning is very clear indeed. The modern world can make 'getting rid' very hard to do. It may seem easier to tolerate their mediocrity, but the message that sends to the rest of the team is pretty toxic. It requires courage and a lot of bullet biting. Get HR advice, follow the process and get rid.

Be a Deviant

Dickheads aside, let's take the concept to the next level. Kim Cameron and Bradley Winn[56] talk about 'virtuous organizations' which are characterized by collective displays of moral excellence by employees. It's the ultimate 'Theory Y' awesomeness, in which they suggest: 'Employees collectively behave in ways that are consistent with the best of the human condition and the highest aspirations of human kind.'

Then Cameron discovered and ran with Gretchen Spreitzer and Scott Sonenshein's notion of 'positive deviance': *'intentional behaviours that depart from the norms of a referent group in honourable ways'*. In simple terms, positively deviant behaviours stand out for all the right reasons.[57]

Just as the key to individual flourishing is to understand and put effort into functioning at our best, so it is within organizations. The traditional leadership focus has been on eliminating weaknesses and solving problems. This is important, but flourishing organizations must go further and, according to Cameron, they must focus on what is 'positively deviant', i.e., what is 'outstanding', what is already working and what is world class. In line with David Cooperrider's work on Appreciative Inquiry[58] this provides a dramatic shift of focus. Organizations need to switch to focusing on the best rather than on the worst. The emphasis falls on strengths, capabilities and possibilities. It doesn't exclude negative events, it learns from them. Thus, you stand a better chance of creating a world class team – one that is flourishing, benevolent, generous and honours people and their contributions.

The grandiose paragraph above doesn't tally with the reality that most organizations are primarily focused on preventing bad things from happening. This distinction is subtle but highly significant. All organizations want excellence, but it is how they go about achieving it that is interesting. As we explained in the 'Love Machine' chapter, the vast majority of organizations are focused on achieving consistency by solving or preventing errors. They put rules/procedures/policies in to achieve minimum standards with the age-old mantra of *this is how you should do things*. It is aimed at stopping mistakes and driven by the fear of failure.

Problem solving is a vitally important skill. It's often high up on any recruiter's list. And yet it has a dark side. We have already talked about sinking into the self-inflicted quagmire of trying to solve everyone else's problems. But there's more. In order to be good at solving problems you need to be good at finding them – and that means that the great problem solvers we prize so highly are often predisposed to focus on what's wrong rather than what's right.

If you've ever worked in manufacturing you will have been on a problem-solving course, maybe even graduating to black-belt of something called 'Six Sigma' (a set of techniques and tools for process improvement introduced by engineer Bill Smith while working at Motorola in 1986, which has turned problem solving into a martial art). The scales are weighed down by negativity because, sadly, there is no corresponding martial art of spotting things that are awesome.

The more we look for what is wrong with our organizations, the more we will find. Every organization has the potential to present a never-ending stream of weaknesses for our attention. Fixing problems is gratifying but, when it becomes a way of life, it is demoralizing and exhausting.

'World class' requires behaviours that extend beyond what is normally expected. In the chart below, normal or healthy performance is at the mid-point with positively and negatively deviant performance at the polar extremes.[59]

Essentially, you can stand out at either end of the spectrum: negative deviance represents eye-wateringly abhorrent deviation from the norm and positive deviance is stand-out amazing.

	Negative deviance	Normal	Positive deviance
Staff wellness	Illness	Health	Vitality
Staff morale	Demoralized	Living for the weekends	Buzzing
Business effectiveness	Struggling	Keeping up – just	World leader
Efficiency	Busy fools	Busy	A busy hive
Quality of output	Insipid	In line with expectations	Wow!
Change readiness	Stuck	Coping	Responsive and anticipatory
Staff engagement	'Presenteeism' (staff are there in body)	A mix of good and bad days	Enthusiasm burns brightly. Staff willingly go the extra mile
Customer engagement	Awkward customers who complain a lot	Indifference. Footloose customers	Customers are raving fans, talking favourably behind your back
'Atmosphere'	Lifeless	Surviving	Flourishing
Leadership style	Controlling. Driven by fear	Empowering (in words only)	Inspiring. Driven by possibilities

Most leaders are driven by the fear of slipping into the negative deviance zone, so become preoccupied with the gap between what is going wrong (mistakes, poorly performing departments, customer complaints, etc.) and the middle point on the continuum. This gap might be labelled a 'deficit gap' or a 'problem solving gap'. A large majority of scientific research in fields such as medicine, psychology and organizational behaviour focuses on deficit gaps such as overcoming problems and grappling with depression, maladies, illness, angry customers, poor quality and under-performing staff.

Often, the gap between the middle (healthy functioning) and the right side (positive deviance) is unexplored. This 'abundance gap' represents the difference between successful and extraordinarily positive performance and is, quite frankly, worthy of some attention. Closing the 'abundance gap' requires that leaders not only focus on being effective, efficient, or reliable in performance, but they also focus on being 'extraordinary'. Close the 'abundance gap' and your stakeholders (staff, customers, suppliers) will be saying 'wow!'

Humans have evolved with a so-called 'negativity bias', a tendency to look at what's not working, suggesting the negative deviance zone is your organization's default position *unless you apply intentional strategies*.

Companies that are renowned for the quality of their customers' experiences have twigged that it's correlated with their employees' experiences. The biggest leverage point for improving the quality of your customers' experiences is the quality of the experience you and your team are having.

It all points to you, the leader. We don't want to get too controversial here but we'd dare to suggest that leadership is the single biggest thing that can make or break your ability to achieve and sustain 'positive deviance'.

Don't Make 'Harder' Your Safe Word

Readers of a certain age will remember the 1980s *Superman* movies in which Christopher Reeve 'Clark Kented' his way through a day job, presumably with lycra briefs in his 'briefcase', using phone boxes as a changing room before swirling around the skies of Metropolis of an evening. Is it a bird? Is it a plane? No it's a terrible whiff of cheesiness. In one particular scene the whiff became a stench. Lois Lane is standing on her balcony when Superman wafts down and lands beside her, shoulders back, jaw jutting, hands on hips. This is the very same guy she shares an office with, yet her powers of investigative reporting or indeed facial recognition, fail her.

Lois, forever the reporter, asks, *'What do you stand for Superman?'*

Our hero raises an eyebrow and announces, *'Truth, justice and the American way.'*

It's scripted halitosis, the equivalent of French brie that's been left in the sun all afternoon. But, however bad the dialogue, at least he knew.

In business, we often confuse 'culture' with 'company values'. You might recall Enron? Their values were 'communication', 'respect', 'excellence' and 'integrity', or at least that's what it said in their company brochure shortly before their executives went to prison for stealing money from their customers. They are an extreme case of 'culture' and 'values' being diametrically opposed.

You can explain corporate values until you're Smurf-faced. But staff don't live by corporate values, they live by their own. We've been at great pains to suggest that to function at its best a team needs to feel connected, as does a family. It's easy to write a set of values and stick them on a poster on the wall under the slogan, *'We genuinely care about our customers'*, but so often the words simply don't match our experience.

How many times have you raged at being left on hold, in cognitive mis-match land with the 'muzak' interspersed with the cheery message: *We know you are waiting and your call is important to us. You are number 84 in the queue. Thank you for holding. Maybe you will find the answer you are looking for on our website.*

Here comes some more hard and soft stuff, this time not skills but measures. 'Hard' objectively defined measures such as sales, customer waiting times, output per hour and customer satisfaction are important. As Jeff Schwartz, CEO of Timberland, states: 'If we don't make money, no amount of virtue will do our firm any good. Wall Street will ignore us, and we will soon be out of business. We must have bottom line performance for virtuousness in our firm to be taken seriously.'[60]

We couldn't agree more. There is no point being a wonderful employer if you can't pay the wages or if you're leaking customers.

If we chuck all the leadership ingredients into a pot, boil it until all the froth has evaporated and we're left with 'essence of pure leadership', what would it be? We think it'd be something to do with leadership being an emotional call to arms. Let's have a peep at an individual emotion and then extrapolate outwards. The relatively stable basic emotional state of 'happiness' refers to the momentary level of happiness that an individual typically experiences – the individual's 'set point'. Basically, although all individuals can experience a range of emotions at different intensities, there is a tendency for these to return to their idiosyncratic 'set point'.

Diener *et al.* (2006)[61] argue that your happiness set point is determined by your sense of identity which is, in turn, determined by your psychology. At its simplest, most people think like the person they perceive themselves to be (for example, victims get stuck in 'learned helplessness', winners have a winning mentality, confident people behave confidently, etc.).

Essentially, Pygmalion, Golem, X & Y also apply in our own heads. We live up or down to the person we think we are. The question therefore arises, is it possible to change one's mental habits and/or sense of personal identity? The concept of neuro-plasticity suggests the brain is always learning and constantly re-wiring itself. Daniel Siegel states that 'Where attention goes, neurons fire. And where neurons fire, they can re-wire' (p. 291).[62] This capacity for the brain to be reconfigured opens up the possibility for genuine and permanent personal change.

What does practice make?

No! Not 'perfect'. *Permanent.*

Practice makes *permanent.*

Neuroplasticity means we're all just a work in progress so, maybe, the message is 'stop trying to be perfect and start trying to be awesome'.

Quick Wins

It's sneaky suspicion time. Most workplaces have targets to reach, so schools are judged on grades, hospitals on waiting times, couriers on deliveries, manufacturers on output per hour, etc. If you're the boss, these targets loom large because you're going to be judged on them. Understandably, you become fixated on your targets.

Free Range Leadership™ (good enough to Trademark)

Even when times are hard I can't possibly ever buy eggs from battery farms. I once watched a TV documentary where they went undercover in a chicken farm. They filmed awful conditions. All very inhumane. The hens are worked around the clock. Minimal appreciation and zero love. The girls are, literally, worked to death. Oh, and the eggs are rubbish.

So I spend a few pence more and get 'free range' because these chooks have been allowed some leeway to stretch their legs, take in some fresh air and feel appreciated. The farmer loves them. Oh, and the eggs are great.

I can't help thinking that 'free range leadership' might also be a good thing?

Our message is this – organizational culture is one of the most important predictors of high levels of performance over time[63] and for 'culture' one should read 'people'. Organizations that flourish have developed a 'culture of abundance' which builds the collective capabilities of all members. Leadership is a lever that should be used to shift the collective emotional and behavioural 'set-point' of the organization and might best be described as a life-giving force, the ability to create energy within an organization. There's no escaping the fact that this 'lever' comes down to emotional intelligence. As a leader, you need to be courageous enough to take your eye off your targets and focus on your people.

Everyone can have a good and bad day. Employees can go through the motions, achieving the bare minimum, clock-watching their way to the end of the day. Equally, they can all choose to give discretionary effort, going above and beyond the minimum requirements. While 'standard' leaders struggle to do this, emotionally intelligent leaders just seem to know. They understand that praise for a job well done (the right amount of praise done in the right way for the right person), or a thank you or donuts on a Friday are all important motivational tools. The 'intelligent' bit is apparent if the leader just does this kind of stuff automatically.

So here are a couple of quick leadership wins. Steve McDermott talks about the 'four-minute rule',[64] suggesting that's how long it takes for other people to catch your emotional state. Taking the example of a meeting, it's eminently doable. You can lose the first four minutes of a meeting, creating stress by whinging about how difficult it's been to organize what with all the pressures and how you're snowed under so aren't properly prepared, before reading out the apologies for people who've got better things to do than attend your meeting, maybe even listing what those 'better things' are: *Sandra's been called to another meeting, Beryl's got a 'situation' to deal with and Clive's son's off with toothache.* Within four minutes you'll have everyone wishing they had come up with an excuse too!

Or you could spend a few minutes thanking everyone for turning up despite the pressures and cultivating a feel-good factor by smiling, praising, creating positivity, celebrating a small success and getting people to feel this is exactly where they want to be for the next 30 minutes. The grapevine will communicate to those who missed the meeting that they really missed out!

Once again, for some the second scenario will seem like the most natural thing in the world. For others, they can feel that option one is more likely.

Another quick win is what Shawn Achor[65] calls the '10/5 principle'. Supplanted from the Ritz-Carlton hotel chain to an American hospital, Achor suggests the simple notion of smiling at anyone who comes within 10 feet and making eye contact and giving a positive greeting to anyone within 5 feet is an example of 'franchising success'. And while sceptics might point to the 10/5 principle as cosmetic, false or, indeed, overly American in tone, Achor reports a different reality. When the behaviour becomes contagious it changes the 'reality' and the feeling of the hospital. Achor reports that staff were smiling and this was 'franchised' to patients and visitors. Crucially, this new behaviour became normalized and embedded in the hospital's culture. To revisit the clunky language from earlier, this simple but powerful habit has changed the cultural set-point.

This really taps into the purity of the leadership goo that sits in the bottom of our pan. What's left after all the froth has been boiled away? What if it's the simple principle that your staff won't do what you say, but will reflect what you do and live up or down to expectations.

No froth folks. If this is what's left in the leadership pan then inspiration truly does have to start very close to home.

Chapter 9

CREATING SUPERHEROES

● ● ● ● ● ●

Ending with a 'chicken or egg' question and starting with presidential 'rule number 6', we manage to sandwich a host of superhero content in-between. We look at a gold medal decathlete and an even more famous scientist, arguing that, in a parallel universe, they'd have led lives of epic failure.

Then it's down to basics – strengths – how to find them and, crucially, how to play to them. Henry Kissinger did it but a banyan tree can't. Then it's off to the land of flow, where output triples, time flies and you get home from work inspired.

Hands up if you want more days like that?

Read on …

Going for Gold

......

'PEOPLE WHO LIVE IN COMFORT ZONES ARE ACTUALLY EXTREMELY UNCOMFORTABLE.'

......

David Taylor

I'm always mad keen on keeping Ben Zander's 'rule number 6' at the forefront of my mind.[66] Zander recounts a story of an American president who was getting very serious and heavy in a meeting with a leader of a foreign nation. His aide approached him and said: *'Mr President Sir, please don't forget rule number 6'.*

The other head of state looked quizzically at the US president and, as you would, he enquired, *'What is rule number 6?'*

And the president beamed and said, *'Rule number 6 is "don't take yourself too seriously".'*

'And the other rules?' enquired the other head of state.

The president's eyes were now twinkling. *'There aren't any,'* he grinned. *'Just rule number 6.'*

And, nice story as it is, it is also a good rule to live your life by. Sure, your career can be a serious business and you've contracted this terrible disease called 'responsibility', but that doesn't mean you have to become deadly serious. A bit of levity helps you swallow the bitter aftertaste of some of life's more unsavoury moments.

We love Richard Wilkins' assertion that we're all superheroes pretending to be normal.[67] If you're ever lucky enough to hear Richard deliver that line, you'll see a twinkle in his eye but you'll realize that he's deadly serious. In business terms, he's very close to the truth. Yes, you might have a couple of staff who are hiding it incredibly well but most folk are capable of amazing things. The leader's job is to tap into their inner superhero and, if you do, it benefits everyone.

But how? Let's take a couple of examples, one from home and one from history.

At a personal level, Andy's daughter had worked really hard at school and came home with a glowing report. Not quite superhero, but it bordered on amazing – grade A predictions across the board, except Science which was a B+. Cue the bunting and cigars? Nope. Her grandma took one look, furrowed her brow and said, *'Ouch! What happened to Science?'* And the moment was gone. I took the bunting down, the cigars were put away for another year and the champagne remained uncorked.

At a 'celebrity' level, *Time* magazine's 'Person of the 20th Century' (1999)[68] would have been consigned to the dustbin of history if we'd focused on his failings. When our celeb was growing up he was referred to as the 'dopey one' and he struggled with words to the point that his family feared he'd never learn to speak. He struggled at school with one teacher telling him he'd never amount to anything and was wasting everyone's time. He muddled through college with uneven grades and struggled to find a job. Our man wanted to be a teacher but it took him fully nine years to land his first teaching job. As if all these weaknesses weren't enough, he was unbelievably absent-minded. Famously, he couldn't remember his own phone number.

This is hardly the stuff of comic books – but of course all we've talked about are his weaknesses. Fortunately, he didn't focus on his weaknesses, but his strengths. Our hero's strength lay in creative thinking – imagining thought experiments that unlocked theoretical physics. Rather than thinking in words, he thought in pictures. He imagined what things would look like if he were to travel on a bullet at the speed of light and whether space might curve, so the distance between two points is not necessarily a straight line.

With his incredible imagination, he helped prove the existence of atoms and developed science's most famous equation: $E = MC^2$. With his brilliant thoughts, he completely revolutionized science.

Of course, we are talking about Albert Einstein, considered by many the greatest genius who ever lived. In 1999, *Time* magazine crowned him the person of the century, describing him as 'the pre-eminent scientist in a century dominated by science'.

So, guess what, Einstein was like you and I – genius at some things and spectacularly bad at others. Fortunately, he worked hard to develop his strengths and didn't let his weaknesses hold him back.

And that's what made him stand head and shoulders above so many others. Sadly, our corporate preoccupation with fixing weaknesses also does a great hatchet job of diminishing the strengths on the other side. It creates a whole load of average automatons and means nobody will be outstanding at anything. Eradicating weaknesses creates middling, run-of-the-mill, Jacks-of-all-trades.

Our starting point is that we're not human beings that are flawed, or problems waiting to be solved; we are potential waiting to unfold. Thrusting your positive best self forward is like putting yeast into the organizational dough.

If we, and those around us, wish to become truly outstanding then the only thing more important than blood, sweat and tears is to play to our strengths. But don't be tempted to thrust this page in your boss's face and say, *'See what it says here. You remember that discussion we had the other day? About my weakness for getting to work on time. This book says you need to learn to live with it and look at my strengths instead.'*

OK, it's simple, but it's not that simple!

Let's apply the learning to Daley Thompson, GB's fabled and moustachioed Olympian who famously whistled his way through the national anthem. For our younger readers Daley won gold in the toughest of all disciplines, the decathlon. Daley was good at nine of the events, yet his muscle-bound frame meant he was ponderously poor at the final event, the 1500m. Fortunately for Daley, he twigged that he would get better results by focusing on the things he was good at. In fact, when it came to the 1500m his aim was merely to get around the track without falling over.

In the corporate world, Daley's personal development plan would have ignored the nine green columns and highlighted that his 1500m times were the thing to focus on. His well-meaning manager would have teed Daley up with some training and he'd have been set next year's SMART target of *'being 2.5 per cent better at 1500m'.*

Daley would have taken his eye off the nine other disciplines, all of which he excelled at. As his efforts moved to achieving marginal gains in the 1500m, his stellar disciplines would slip and, hence, Daley stops shining. We suspect Daley might have given up on the decathlon altogether and taken up professional whistling?

The analogy sounds crazy, but we see it happening every day in well-meaning but misguided teams. 'Competency frameworks' are our bugbear. Quit trying to get everyone to be competent in everything, and if you have to use a competency framework then use it to build strengths. Yes, if your weaknesses are stopping you working safely or massively hindering you, sort them. But we promise that as soon as you acknowledge and accept them, and switch your focus to your strengths, you'll achieve giant leaps of learning.

Fact

At the height of his powers, the legendary and fearsome West Indian fast bowler, Tino Best, had an answerphone message that went: *'This is Tino Best speaking, the fastest bowler in the world. I can't take your call right now but I'll get back to you as soon as I've practised how to get faster.'*

Whistling in the Wind

Donald Clifton and James Harter[69] make the point that providing feedback on weaknesses is also important but that a focus on deficiencies leads only to the development of competence whereas a focus on strengths leads to excellence and positively deviant performance. In other words, if we focus on what's wrong we create a world of grey where everyone is average, but if we focus on what's right then we create a world of brilliant colour where different people stand out and excel in different ways.

However, for most of us, getting to know our strengths is a big hurdle. As Marcus Buckingham and Donald Clifton articulate: 'The real tragedy of life is not that each of us doesn't have enough strengths, it's that we fail to use the ones we have' (p. 9).[70] Remember, it's all too common to become enormously familiar with our weaknesses and uncomfortably inarticulate with our strengths. For those of us who don't know how to identify strengths, where can we start?

Your recent experience is a great place to start. If you have a diary or calendar you can start there, otherwise grab a coffee and have a quick trip down memory lane. Reflect on the last two weeks and notice when you were last 'in the zone' or as Sir Ken Robinson calls it, 'in your element'. You'll be able to distinguish these moments as those where your sense of time disappeared and you felt completely engaged.

Time to take notes. What were you doing in that moment? Don't worry about who was there, why you were there and the peripheral stuff. Concentrate on what you were doing and make detailed notes. When you're 'in the zone' you are using a strength and the more you understand what your strengths are, the more you can bring them into play. So identify the strength(s) you were using and make a note. Now trawl back a bit further and repeat for other moments. The more strengths you identify the more opportunities you will have to use them.

We can play the same game going forward. Look at what's coming up in the next few weeks and identify the stuff you are really looking forward to. Which days will you be jumping out of bed with a bound because of what you've got planned? Make notes about those exciting things and think about why those future events energize you.

Ok. You may want to take a break before the next one. We'd like you to do a full time travel back through your history. Not in detail and it's not a life flashing before your eyes thing, unless you're reading this while plummeting to your death. If you do happen to be plummeting to your death at this point: 1. We are really sorry to hear that; 2. We are honoured that anyone would spend their last moments on this beautiful planet reading our humble little tome; 3. Stop reading it and remember all those beautiful moments in your life.

Back in the room. So you're doing a whistle stop tour of your life in a non-terminal way. Notice the stuff you took to easily and picked up naturally. The jobs or skills you just got first time, like you were made to do it. Look across your learning, work and social history. What comes naturally to you? Write it down.

Some of you may be reading this thinking: *I don't keep diaries and I don't do ferreting about in my past that well and I'm not currently plummeting to my death (phew!).* In which case just start noticing and making a note going forward.

The next step is to look at your notes and tease out the common themes. It can really help to talk through your notes with someone who knows you well and spends a fair bit of time with you. They'll be able to point out the things you are great at but only you will be able to identify the energizing activities that captivate you.

Go through your notes and identify your top five strengths. Make a note of them. The next step is simple. *Use them.* Now that you know your strengths you can focus on how you can use them more across your life to do the things you need to do. The more you use your strengths, the more energized you will feel and the happier you will be, like the proverbial pig in shit.

If your job doesn't automatically lend itself to your strengths, have a conversation with your manager and see whether it can be accommodated. You, your team and your manager will benefit if they give you work that plays to your strengths.

Marcus Buckingham suggests that only two out of ten people get to use their strengths every day.[71] Imagine if it was seven out of ten – or even higher? What would that do in terms of results AND engagement? Learning from the previous three sentences:

1. Make sure that, in your team, at least 7 out of 10 people get to use their strengths every single day.

2. If you're not currently the leader and hence cannot influence things as much as you'd like, make sure you're one of the 2 out of 10, the minority who get to play to their strengths on a daily basis.

Team Strengths

Once you have a team-based view of key strengths, you will be in a great position to optimize the work across the team to get the best out of all members. When you do that, connection, engagement and productivity will rocket because you are recognizing what your team loves and giving them what they do best. Having this level of team understanding allows you to partner colleagues up where there is a synergy of strengths to deliver an outcome.

There are no downsides.

Alternatively or additionally, get your team to undertake the process of 'reflective best self' in which employees ask their colleagues to write three short anecdotes in response to the question: *When you have seen me make a special or important contribution, what unique value did I create?* The answers should provide a raft of positive feedback as well as an insight into the employee's personal strengths. The aim is for the individual to analyse the feedback and devise strategies to make better use of these strengths.

But before you get too carried away, be mindful that the world doesn't give a stuff whether you use your strengths or not, it just wants you and your team to deliver. It's your responsibility to make sure that the team delivers in a way that allows the team members to use their strengths.

We believe that playing to your strengths makes such a difference to the quality of your working life that if there isn't enough flexibility in the role for you to use your strengths – then it's high time to go and look for something else!

Thought for the day …

There's a cool Yogic metaphor about the banyan tree, which is common across south Asia. The banyan tree has a main trunk but, as it grows, it sets a whole system of new trunks that become indistinguishable from the original. This means the banyan tree is able to grow outwards and upwards, arching far and wide, blocking the light and creating shade for the people and animals.

That's all well and good but the by-product of this protection is that nothing can grow underneath the banyan tree.

Think on.

Going With the Flow

The truth is that we all have our version of Daley Thompson's 1500m at work – tasks we have to get on with but are rubbish at. The good news is that we have more choice than a decathlete. Maybe the event isn't core to your role and doesn't have to be done? Maybe someone else could do it – someone for whom that particular task is a strength. Or maybe, after looking at all other options, you just need to get on with it and get it done? Either way it is critical to take responsibility for managing our weaknesses – without making them the primary focus of our attention.

The challenge in most organizations is that performance management policies and processes and the terminology all focus on making you mediocre, not bad, fair to middling. The term 'weakness' has been replaced by 'development need' and a lot of you will be familiar with being offered a 'development opportunity' by your boss, which you both knew was code for a rubbish task that you would hate doing.

Making 'weakness' a dirty word and focussing on eliminating them is like setting the Sat Nav for 'Shitsville', because that's where your organization will end up. Throw in competence frameworks, satisfaction surveys, service level agreements and SMART objectives and you are guaranteed to create an achingly mediocre environment.

In Mike's last organization, if someone was having a bad day they would say *'I'm off to the roof to toss myself off'*. Yes, there are a couple of ways you can interpret that. The point being that a focus on 'development needs' will end up with the employees flocking to the roof and that could be very messy for your organization (yes, we know, two ways again, neither very pleasant).

When you're looking at your strengths, make sure you focus on your true strengths. You're probably good at a whole load of stuff, but your true strengths will be those that you love doing and energize you when you're using them. This is really important as you need to have that passion and energy, otherwise you won't put in the time to practise. When you are using a true strength, you'll feel energized and alive and be able to just keep going. You'll lose track of time and get lost in the moment. When you use your strengths at work the day will fly by and you'll leave more energized than when you arrived.

True story …

A member of Henry Kissinger's team once wrote him a report. Kissinger sent a note asking, *'Is this your best work?'*

'No sir,' came the reply, *'I can do better.'*

Two weeks later, the new improved report landed on Kissinger's desk. Once again, the employee received a note saying, *'Seriously, is this the best you can do?'*

Fearing something was amiss, the team member responded, *'No sir, I'm sure I can do better,'* and one week later a new report landed on Kissinger's desk, this time was a hand-written note saying, *'Mr K, I promise this is my very best work.'*

Kissinger sent an immediate reply saying, *'In that case sir, this time I shall read it.'*

That's what is so great about playing to your strengths – not only are you performing at your peak when you use your strengths, you are absolutely 100 per cent engaged. In fact, we believe that getting people to identify and play to their strengths is the single biggest thing that you can use to rocket employee engagement. And it doesn't cost a penny. It just requires a bit of a rethink.

At its upper end, engagement has been referred to as 'flow' or the overall feeling referred to as 'being in the zone'. 'Flow' and 'strengths' are a bit 'chicken and egg'. We're not sure which comes first but you can't have one without the other. You don't need expensive trips abroad to motivate your team, you just need to get them doing what they love – and the rest will take care of itself.

To finish this chapter, how about we put our feet up and let Richard Branson take the strain. He's done alright for himself and seems, by all accounts, to be held up as a leadership role model. Here's a Branson Top Ten:

Tip #1 Listen more than you talk. Nobody learned anything by hearing themselves speak.

Tip #2 Three steps to success: Hire great talent, give them the tools to succeed, and get out of the way.

Tip #3 Train people well enough so they can leave, treat them well enough so they don't want to.

Tip #4 It is only by being bold that you get anywhere. If you are a risk-taker, then the art is to protect the downside. The brave may not live forever but the cautious do not live at all.

Tip #5 Have courage. Courage is what it takes to stand up and speak; courage is also what it takes to sit down and listen.

Tip #6 I never get the accountants in before I start up a business. It's done on gut feeling, especially if I can see that they are taking the mickey out of the consumer.

Tip #7 You don't learn to walk by following rules. You learn by doing, and by falling over. One thing is certain in business. You and everyone around you will make mistakes.

Tip #8 There is no greater thing you can do with your life and your work than follow your passions – in a way that serves the world and you. As soon as something stops being fun, I think it's time to move on. Life is too short to be unhappy.

Tip #9 Fun is at the core of the way I like to do business and it has been key to everything I've done from the outset. More than any other element, fun is the secret of Virgin's success.

Tip #10 If somebody offers you an amazing opportunity but you are not sure you can do it, say yes – then learn how to do it later!

The gospel according to Sir Richard. #Amen.

Chapter 10

CLIMB EVERY MOUNTAIN

● ● ● ● ● ●

This chapter is an epic climb to the top of the highest mountain, showing that you can begin climbing even at the ripe old age of 73.

We come full circle to Taylorism, showing that 150 years down the line, time and motion is alive and well, squeezing the life out of everyone it touches. Ironically, we even manage to measure 'bottom wiping', surely the most immeasurable motion of them all?

We dare to tear SMART apart, suggesting that all teams need a HUGG instead. We check out a school that cancelled Christmas on the grounds of technical efficiency, suggesting that leaders sometimes make things extra hard.

Speaking of extra hard, that mountain won't get climbed just by looking up at it. Boots and crampons on, up we go …

Technical Efficiency

We all have deeper yearnings. Even professions where you'd expect an in-built sense of caring can have their passion extinguished. Nurses can end up jaded, teachers can end up disliking children – you can see it in their eyes. The relentless nature of the system is beating the humanity and caring out of the natural carers. If teachers think that ticking Ofsted boxes is their priority, they will lose their mojo. If doctors think that keeping waiting lists down is their *raison d'être*, they will stop caring.

Recent media examples bear this out. When a care worker is allocated 15 minutes per home visit it screams 'efficiency' and 'cost saving' as top priorities. F. W. Taylor's good old fashioned 'time and motion' has barged in through the back door of the caring professions. 'Dressing a wound' (10 minutes), 'bathing' (12 minutes), 'wiping someone's bottom' (1 minute), 'getting an old person dressed' (4 minutes)... this might make sense at some sort of scientific level where, technically, everything can be measured, costed and accounted for, but it falls down on lots of levels, most notably from the customer and staff experience. From the care receiver's view, every so often a harried new face will pop in, do the basics in a whirlwind of busyness and rush out of the door. From the care giver's perspective, the system spits out a list of 'customers' at the start of the day, a list that is so long and unachievable that their heart sinks before they've even started.

If we transplant the same leadership crassness to call centre workers, we find they're often measured on calls per hour. This technical imperative means they deal with clients as quickly as possible – the subtext being that we value speed over quality. Maybe a slightly longer call would result in better customer retention?

In both examples, the 'system', in its technically efficient glory, has failed to take account of the fact that the staff and customers are human beings, with feelings and drives. Have you ever tried to measure happiness, positivity, empathy, courage or caring? Because, you see, whatever your 'system', it grinds to a halt without them.

If we follow through on the example above, the technical efficiency of the system results in more old people receiving sub-standard care and being re-admitted to hospital and your new-fangled efficiency savings have ended up costing more.

Look around and you'll see it ...

······

'EVER MORE PEOPLE TODAY HAVE THE MEANS TO LIVE, BUT NO MEANING TO LIVE FOR.'

······

Viktor Frankl

We are not really railing against the system, merely hinting that there might be a better way. And that 'better way' can't happen without genuine employee engagement which, in turn, doesn't stand a chance unless we have engaged leaders who are willing (and able) to shift their thinking.

Of course, it's always a fine balance between asking too much or too little of your staff. The majority expect (indeed want) to work hard. As do you. The balance is for them and you to live on the edges of your ability. Let's call it being 'whelmed'; not under- or overwhelmed, but living in a state of perfect whelm.

So far so good. But there's more.

Tenzing and Hillary

We think it's fair to say that all the previous chapters have focused on connection and potential. That's because leadership is all about 'people' and people are driven entirely by emotions. Indeed, it's emotion that creates motion. Get the right people fully engaged, and success is inevitable. But success at what? Once you have got the right people on the bus in the right seats, what next?

It's about the classic Henry Ford quote about everyone going forward together. If you want that to happen everyone needs to know what direction to go in. Yes folks, the moment has arrived. No leadership book on the planet is complete without a section on goal setting.

No. No! Stop yawning. We're going to do it differently.

We touched on it in Chapter 9 when we were looking at recrafting jobs to suit our strengths. The two questions to ask to clarify a goal are: *What do you want?* and *How will you know when you've got it?* You can use these questions to shape just about any goal but, before you do, there's something really important to sort out. You need to know where you are right now.

It's worth remembering that *Where are we now?* And *Where are we going?* aren't one-time questions or something to be updated annually. The world and your organization are constantly evolving, so the wise leader will always know where the team and organization is and how the future landscape is changing so that they can stay on course. Too many so-called leaders have set off on an epic journey of organizational change and achieved it – only to find they've been changing in the wrong direction.

When it comes to setting goals too many leaders get bogged down with SMART. If ever an acronym needed a makeover, it's this one. Yes, we can agree with Specific, Measurable and Timebound, but Realistic and Achievable? Really? These are the Bridget Jones knickers of goal-setting. If you want to kill the passion in your team, set them a target that is like last year's, but just a little bit higher. As I type these words my nostrils are flaring as I stifle a yawn.

Here's the truth. If you want to be like every other team in your organization, set yourself some SMART objectives. If you want to be exactly the same as your competitors, ditto. A better description would be Pathetic, Insipid, Sedentary and Same as last year goals but we've a similar acronymic problem that we encountered with TOSS.

If you want to be truly world class, we advocate that you take a bit of a gamble, go against the tide of traditional management thinking and set massive goals. We call them Huge Unbelievably Great Goals, or HUGGs. A HUGG is something that is currently out of reach – you have to grow, innovate and engage in order to achieve it. A HUGG is on the edges of achievability but it's not out of sight. It might be that you only get half way there – but your achievements will reach far beyond *a little bit better than last year*. A HUGG isn't something to be afraid of – it's something to aspire to.

Bowing once more to the fabulous Kim Cameron, he talks about the concept of 'Everest goals' and the clue's in the name.[72] Has Mount Everest ever been conquered? *Yup.* But only by a committed few. In a corporate setting, Everest goals are positively deviant in that they are not just designed to overcome problems and achieve success, but to reach extraordinary high levels of performance, which Cameron and Marc Levine[73] define as performance that spectacularly and dramatically exceeds normal. Further, such goals are focused on 'goods of first intent' (i.e. the goal 'is good in itself and is to be chosen for its own sake').[74]

Thought for the day …

Your dream is watching you, it's calling you. *'Come get me, I'm over here.'*

Are you going to pursue it or stand and admire it?

Let's give you an example. Andy was recently doing some work with a senior leadership team in a school. Despite working themselves to near exhaustion, the school results were muddling through on 39 per cent A to C grades, the benchmark being 50. The head was troubled by their inability to get out of 'special measures', a suffocating category created by the school inspectorate, to indicate a severe arse-kicking. Ironically, in school report terms, it is very much 'could do much better'. 'Special measures' means the pressure is really on and this school had battened down the hatches and was squeezing extra work out of everyone and monitoring performance so you couldn't go for a shit without filling in a form. That might be an exaggeration but I promise you this bit is true, the head had cancelled Christmas on the grounds that, *'It's not a priority like maths or English, but good news...'* she croaked as I peered into her bloodshot eyes, *'...it looks like it's all been worthwhile because results have improved from 39 to 41.8 per cent'.*

Her smile was weak and mine non-existent. She'd fallen into the age-old trap of doing the same, but harder.

'So what's the best school in this city achieving?' Andy asked.

'Oh, well they have a different catchment,' she began. *'They have supportive parents ...'*

'... And what are they achieving?' (I deliberately butted in to head off her excuses at the pass.)

'84 per cent,' she said. *'But...'*

'So what are you going to do to beat them?'

Because, you see, I genuinely think that's an exciting question. It's not coming at the future from the past, it's looking at the future through a different lens – the lens of *How awesome do we want to be?* rather than *How rubbish are we right now?*

Cutting to the chase, the leadership team reframed their goals, away from SMART and towards HUGGs. Eighteen months later their results were 24 percentage points higher – and as the head said, *'Not yet the best in the city, but we're snapping at their heels'.*

So let's leave you with two messages about goals. If you want to be inspired as a leader and for your people to be inspired as well, your goals need to be inspiring, awesome HUGGs. Are you really going to bounce into work in the morning pumped up and excited about increasing productivity by 2 per cent over the next two quarters? Nope, didn't think so. Inspired people need HUGGs.

The key to making those HUGGs a reality is to take the time to rethink how you're going to get there. Your current actions got you to where you are, working a bit harder could get you that 2 per cent performance improvement, but getting close to your HUGGs needs new thinking and action, the sort of thinking and action which an inspired team will relish the opportunity to generate.

Cutting to the chase, we can't think of anyone who's ever changed the world by fitting in. Look around. They're playing SMART. We encourage you to go large.

Gandhi

Attila the Hun

Jesus

Steve Jobs

Hitler

What do these guys have in common?

Chapter 11

WHY YOUR 'WHY-FACTOR' IS ACTUALLY YOUR 'X-FACTOR'

• • • • • •

Gosh, a chapter heading that makes your head hurt! And it's a biggy in magnitude of themes.

We ask what have Gandhi and Hitler got in common, before introducing you to the world's greatest leader and then dare to suggest it ties in rather nicely with Simon Sinek's concept of the golden circle.

We follow up with a bit of basic brain stuff and hammer the point that purpose trumps pay almost every time.

We finish with a big question: *Are you worth signing up to?*

While you ponder that, we'll get cracking...

Lift-Off

······

'MOST OF THE SHADOWS OF THIS LIFE ARE CAUSED BY OUR STANDING IN OUR OWN SUNSHINE.'

······

Ralph Waldo Emerson

Hurtling towards the end of the book, the message so far is overwhelmingly simple – make sure your team has the potential to succeed – that's a heady mix of the right skills, knowledge, mind-set and motivation. You need to listen, coach and build strengths. Your aim is to create a team that does not rely upon you to do the thinking for them, and one that takes 100 per cent responsibility for results whether you are there or not. Set the coordinates for 'huge goals', get excited and it's chocks away.

Or is it?

We think there's one more crucial piece before lift-off. One thing that will lighten the load and make it easier for your team to fly. Another 'thing' that can be couched in riddles as *simple but not easy* and *definitely not actually a thing*.

Cutting to Andy's research one last time, income is way down the list of priorities for flourishing employees. Indeed, the biggest motivator for flourishing employees is *making a difference*. People have a strong desire to find meaning in their work and, if they can, they are more likely to be engaged. Once engaged, there ensues a host of benefits such as enhanced wellbeing, attendance, profit, customer satisfaction, shareholder return and business growth. The practical implications are that organizational structures, leadership styles and job-design can be used to create an environment where employee engagement is more likely, but it is not a guarantee.

There's a correlation between wellbeing and meaning, but not causation. That means feeling good doesn't cause you to have meaning, but having meaning does cause you to feel good. So maybe human beings are driven to find meaning?

What if meaning's the pot of emotional gold we're searching for and happiness comes as part of the package? (The question mark is Andy thinking aloud. That has much bigger connotations than a single sentence should ever have. Plus, it partly explains the God thing.)

Before we plunge headlong into 'purpose', Andy has a hunch that there's an item in the pecking order that comes above wellbeing and meaning? This factor that trumps them is so lovely – it's called *'being a good person'*.

Because, you see, you can be happy and have a very strong meaning, but be a very bad person. For example, some of the Nazis went about their job with a smile, and boy, did they have a cause they believed in.

But what utter bastards.

Fix-It Leadership™

We've sat through so many tired leadership seminars when delegates have to make a list of great leaders. The usual suspects are trotted out; in the good corner we get Churchill, Jobs, Branson, Gates, Gandhi, Martin Luther King and, in the bad corner: Thatcher, Hitler and Attila the Hun. Indeed, the 'great man' theory is supported in that they're almost all men. There's an argument as to whether the last two were 'great leaders' and someone usually counter-balances Hitler with Jesus.

······

'WITH GREAT POWER COMES GREAT RESPONSIBILITY.'

······

Ben Parker (Spider-Man's uncle,
Spider-Man, *2002)*

And the discussion goes round in circles. They all had followers, which is pretty much the only thing they had in common. You could argue that they all had a vision. But it's a raging certainty that they all had a big dollop of luck and, crucially, they all fitted the situation at the time. If you mixed and matched them, I doubt they'd have had so many followers? For example, if you'd put Gandhi in charge of 1930s Germany? A different result for sure, and a very different dress code! Or stick Jesus as chief exec of Virgin or Attila the Hun at Apple? Or even, as history tells us, put Churchill in charge of non-war Britain, it all turns out a bit pants.

We'd like to throw another name into the mix, a modern-day superhero, someone who transcends the genre. Bear with us while we revisit 1976 to gather our evidence ...

In those heady days of the 70s, we had very limited choice of TV channels but were endowed with an inspiring array of superheroes. I could wax lyrical about Flash Gordon, The Hulk and (especially) Wonder Woman, but I'll reserve my hero worship for the greatest 70s superhero of them all, Steve Austin, a man barely alive and whom they rebuilt for a measly six million dollars. But these superheroes had a TV series for a reason – because they were special. If you upset Bruce Banner he'd go green and throw you about, Wonder Woman had amazing child-bearing hips, and The Six Million Dollar man had bionic legs, arm and a special eye. (Apparently the first draft 'man' had two bionic arms and one leg but a superhero that runs in a circle very fast and is a very good hopper was never going to impress).

Fast-forward to the early 2000s and my son started watching *Bob the Builder*. I doff my hat to all the builders in the land because they possess skills I haven't got, but I struggled to see why Bob had a TV series. As far as I could see, he was a regular guy who went around doing his job. Sure, he did it with a smile on his face and he was more upbeat than any of the real-life builders I know, but I couldn't see that he warranted a TV series? It's not as though Bob had had an accident with a rivet gun when he was five that'd turned him into the 'contractor of choice'.

So why was my son transfixed? There was only one thing for it. I sat down with my lad and watched an episode (season 1, episode 8 in case you're interested) in which Scoop notices that Farmer Pickles has entered Scruffty into the dog show, which makes him determined to also enter Pilchard, even though she is a cat. First thing to note is that there's very little building work cracking off but, when it does, Bob and his team sing and dance their way through every job. That is a joy in itself. But the best bit is that when the shit hits the fan – which it invariably does – Bob doesn't jack it in and stomp off home moaning about how bad his day's been. Instead, when things go belly-up Bob shouts to his team, 'Can we fix it?' and his team shout back, 'Yes we can!'

That was it for me. We rewound that bit and watched it again. I mouthed it to myself as Bob shouted. 'Can we fix it?'

'Yes we can!'

What's more, I noticed it was his team shouting 'Yes we can!' as though Bob was some sort of empowering leader.

'Does he always say that?' I asked my son.

'Yes dad,' he said. 'Every job goes over time and over budget. I don't think he makes much money. I mean, last week he had to re-tarmac Mrs Scoggin's driveway, twice, because they'd tarmacked over the keys to his van. But he's very positive about it. He loves being a builder and everyone loves being in his team.'

So, here's a thought for you. It might just be that Bob's your ultimate modern-day leader – an ordinary guy in most respects in that he's got the same van, same tools and been to the same college and got the same City & Guilds level 3 as all the other builders. What marks Bob out as extraordinary is the attitude that he carries around with him. People want to be on Bob's team and, to push the thinking beyond its cartoony limits, we'd suggest that Bob's attitude makes him the best builder in the world.

Bob's attitude is what we call his 'portable benefit' – he brings it with him. Tarmacking over your van keys is not ideal. And finding that one of your work colleagues has entered his cat into a dog show is a sign that some of his team are a sandwich short of a picnic. Yes, he'd fail on the 'No Dickheads' policy but massively gain on the 'be a nice person' criterion. Bob is enlightened to the point that he knows he can't control the external world. He can fire off a final written warning to whichever team member did the tarmacking or he could sack whomever recruited the village idiot, but that's not Bob's way.

Bob's attitude not only makes him the best builder in the world, I would go as far as saying he is a superhero for modern times – ordinary guy, *extra*-ordinary attitude. He is indeed standing on the edge of what's possible.

It just so happens Bob has built a thriving business driven by customers who are raving fans.

The lesson for me was obvious. Bob's in charge of his attitude. It's in his head. His attitude is his portable benefit. If Bob can do it, so can I. And if I can do it, so can you.

If your team are truly connected AND they have what it takes then whichever direction you point them in, they are likely to succeed. But, of course, Bob's not real. So that story doesn't count. *Or does it?*

The Best Habit

The degree to which a leader can affect technical performance has been substantially overstated. But the importance of moral leadership has been greatly underappreciated.

Management thinking …

'Planning fallacy' is a law of business that states we're lousy at figuring out how much time something will take to complete. It results from a heady combination of overestimating our abilities and underestimating the degree to which we're overestimating.

Here's how organizations happen. They grow to a point where the leaders have to relinquish some control. Inevitably, someone messes up so some rules and policies are invented to create control and order. It reduces the risk of someone else doing something stupid. Over time, new rules are added until everyone becomes strangled in expenses forms, dress codes, IT protocols, service level agreements, email disclaimers, internet usage policies, appraisal documentation, person specs and ISO documentation. Next, you need managers to monitor the policies and create an audit trail of compliance and before you know it, the organization has become a cold-blooded serial killer, the chalked-outlines of innovation, inspiration, deviation, excitement, risk and creativity littering your office floor.

I remember learning that the combustion engine is only 30 per cent efficient. It's so frustrating that all that fuel you put into your car gets lost in heat and noise. Organizations are kind of the same. Sure, everyone's working hard – in fact, there's a ridiculous amount of effort – but is there too much friction, heat and noise? (On an unrelated topic, I note that in a recent Gallup survey, employee engagement is also 30%. Maybe it's not unrelated?)

> Scary and true ...
>
> Give a chimp a banana and it will eat the banana.
> Give a chimp a lot of bananas and it will share them.
> Give a chimp a room full of bananas and it will kill other chimps to protect them.

Brace yourself. Here's some controversy. Somewhat counter-intuitively, we strongly advocate that you start putting your customers second. Yes, *second!*

Employees must always come first, because that way they'll put the customer first. It's nigh on impossible to have raving fans if you haven't got raving staff.

Applying a modicum of academia, positive meaning has been proposed as a universal human need[75] and 'making a difference' features as the main motivator in Andy's thesis. If we ratchet the academia up a notch, Charles O'Reilly and Jennifer Chatman[76] propose three types of employee/organization relationships: compliance, identification and internalization:

- **Compliance** produces the desired behaviours through punishment and rewards. Employees conform to norms, not because they want to, but because the rewards and punishment system demands that they do. These tend to be employees who see themselves as having nothing more than a 'job'.
- **Identification** relationships are closely allied to employees with a 'career' orientation who tend to be committed to the organization and seek involvement, producing mutually beneficial results for the employee and their employer.
- **Internalization** is defined by complete absorption of the organization's goals resulting in unequivocal loyalty and pro-social behaviours. An internalized relationship is less dependent on the nature of the work and more dependent on the meaningfulness attached by the employee. These people are likely to view their work as a 'calling'.

Remember Teal from Chapter 2? We dropped it in, early doors, and because it was a bit radical, we ran away and left it hanging. Now we're brave enough to come full circle, from the bad old days when work was to be endured, to the good new days when work needs to be aligned with your purpose.

••••••

FEAR IS WETTING YOUR PANTS. COURAGE IS DOING WHAT YOU HAVE TO DO. WITH WET PANTS.

••••••

Dan Sullivan

How times have changed. In 'Meet the Millennials' Leigh Buchanan puts it like this: 'One of the characteristics of Millennials, besides the fact that they are masters of digital communication, is that they are primed to do well by doing good. Almost 70 per cent say that giving back and being civically engaged are their highest priorities.'[77]

In contemporary society, it's no longer just about a good job in a profitable company – employees want to have a positive impact on the world around them. Yet recent research conducted by YouGov revealed 37 per cent of working British adults say their job is not making a meaningful contribution to the world.[78]

Leaders who help people close the gap on meaning will be able to inspire their organizations not simply to deliver, but to thrive. Especially so if they create a purpose that is not just meaningful but significant. For example, the leaders can reframe work to highlight the positive impact it has on others. Richard Hackman and Greg Oldman discovered that employees who were aware of the positive impact of their contribution had a significantly higher level of meaningfulness. That's why it's such a good idea to reconfigure workplaces so employees interact directly with those receiving their output or service.[79]

Researchers have long recognized the motivational potential of 'task significance'[80] yet many employees never have the chance to see or meet the people affected by their work. Adam Grant studied call centre workers who improved their productivity by 400 per cent after meeting their customers.[81] Thus, seeing the impact of your work can be a powerful source of intrinsic motivation by building meaning into the job.

Thus, the final piece of our leadership jigsaw, after 'connection' and 'potential' is 'reason', or as Simon Sinek calls it, your 'why?' He poses some knee-trembling questions: *What's your purpose? What's your cause? What's your belief? Why does your organization exist? Why do you get out of bed in the morning?* And the biggest one of all: *Why should anyone care?*[82]

If you haven't got a clear 'why?' for your organization then how can you expect people to care? How can you make sure you attract and keep the right people? How can you make sure you deliver? Think about it – what's your 'why'? And remember, 'profit' is a result, not a 'why'.

As Sinek argues, every person, team and organization knows *what* they do; some even know *how* they do it, in other words what makes you/them different from the competition, your USP. Very few – in fact only the inspired few, have the *why-factor*.

Your 'why?' isn't about making a living or even making a profit – it's about a higher purpose that acts as a guiding light in everything you do. Sinek's point is that the stronger an individual employee's 'why?' the more likely their internal motivational boiler will be belting out energy.

The 'Golden Circle', based on Sinek (2011, p. 37)

Where a sense of purpose is lacking or weak, it may be that the leader's role is in helping teams and individuals find a strong and compelling reason why. It's motivational rocket fuel. Working hard for something we don't care about is called stress. Working hard for something we love is called passion.

But of course, the 'why' question starts much closer to home. It's worth pointing the finger back at yourself and asking: *Why do you do what you do?*

It's a question your author tag-team have all pondered prior to leaving corporate life and striding out to create alternative careers. Let's take Jonathan's story.

At the start of my journey I was constantly being asked what I did, and every time I found myself giving the same glib response – *'I'm a coach, trainer, facilitator and consultant'* – and every time I heard myself say it, I had the same sinking feeling inside. I was like every other self-employed trainer and my answer was so dull that I was boring myself to death. So I went on a journey (no, not to mystical monastery in Nepal where I sat cross-legged for three weeks, eating locusts and chanting mantras; it was a journey in my head that required nothing more than quiet and serious contemplation) to move away from *what* I did and *how* I did it, to understand my own personal reasons for doing it. *Why* was I a coach, trainer, facilitator and consultant?

I don't need to share my *why* with you. The important thing is that I have nailed what it is and if you were to bump into me now and ask the very same question, I would give you a very different answer. Strangely, *what* I actually do hasn't changed, it's just how I communicate it. It gets a very different reaction from the people I engage with and, best of all, it gives me a shiver down my spine every time I say it (so if you meet me in Sainsbury's, please do ask!)

In these times where change is constant and everything's on the up except your budget – a team with a clear 'why' is not just nice-to-have, it's an absolutely-must-have. It will turbo-charge discretionary effort.

••••••

'EITHER WALK INTO WORK A LEGEND OR MAKE AN EXCUSE AND TRY AGAIN TOMORROW.'

••••••

Tweet from dave_resource

This is where we depart from psychology and bring in some biology. When both you and your team know your *why-factor* (personal or otherwise), you are talking to them on a very different level and to a different part of their brain – the bit that makes their decisions for them.

Your brain is an amalgam of jelly, two bits of which are vital to explaining your *why-factor*. Firstly, there's the neo-cortex: the rational, logical, thinking part of your brain. Daniel Kahneman calls it system 2, and it deals with all types of analysis, working out *what* you should do.[83]

The limbic system, and particularly the amygdala, is part of system 1, a much quicker instinctive part of your brain. It deals in emotional currency and acts as the gate-keeper for system 2. Sometimes things happen that trigger such a strong emotional response that your amygdala hijacks the situation and cuts system 2 off. For example, if you're speeding along on a wet motorway and brake lights appear through your blurry windscreen blades, you don't rational-ize, *I wonder if I should be applying the brakes?* Your foot is slammed to the floor and you stop just in time, heart-racing in case there's a collision and you need to react.

This visceral reaction is your limbic system and it's might-ily speedy, in fact five times faster than your thinking brain.

So when you communicate starting from your *why-factor* it creates very different feelings than if you articulated from your *what-factor.* Recalling from earlier that emotion creates motion – how you feel determines your behaviour – having a clear and compelling reason for doing something is the best place to start.

Applied to leadership, if you have people who believe what you believe, they will trust you with any product development or pricing policy – because they want what you produce.

Think of an example of a business where you don't understand their *why-factor* so the only way for them to get your loyalty is to manipulate you into a purchase or decision. Remember your last visit to the supermarket when you bought brand X because it was reduced or on a buy-one-get-one-free deal, and on your next visit it was back to full price so you didn't buy it and bought an alternative instead?

If your team either don't know what you stand for, or if they do but you don't believe in the same things, it's pretty much impossible for them to be inspired by you. So you'll have to resort to manipulation to get them to deliver, usually incentives or bonuses.

Manipulation works, but it's not a one-time thing. Once you start you need to keep doing it because it's the only thing motivating your team/organization to deliver. We don't think leadership is about manipulation. We said right at the start that it is about being inspired and the only way you can really be inspired is if you are aligned to your purpose, your 'why'. When you are you can go for it all guns blazing and, when your team share that 'why' they'll be going for it with you. If what you're doing is a little off-purpose, you'll know it, the team will know it and it will be harder to deliver, simply because none of you really believe in it.

If I'm working on something that enables me to live my *why-factor* then I'm in it hook line and sinker – I can stand in front of workshops full of people and I'd be there all night if they let me because it's my calling.

So what's your *why-factor*? If you can connect with your purpose you'll find yourself feeling rather like Bob the Builder, glowing with creativity, positivity and ideas. You are in tune with what you care about and where you're going. Best of all, you inspire others. And, of course, it doesn't mean you won't encounter setbacks, roadblocks or idiots. You'll come face to face with apathy and resistance but you'll be creative in how you handle them. When someone tarmacs over your van keys you'll bounce back. You'll have more uptime than downtime.

We've gone to great lengths to suggest leadership is not about competencies, skills or personality. Well, go on then, maybe a little bit. But we think it's less about inspiring people or trying to motivate them and much more about being inspired. And that comes from being in touch with your passion and then going for it. So questions such as: *What do I care about?, What matters to me?, What do I value the most?* will give some clues as to what lights your internal fire.

Ben Zander calls it being enrolled,[84] as in '*yep, sign me up for that, it sounds exciting*'.

Hence the biggest question in the entire book may well be this one: *Are you worth signing up to?*

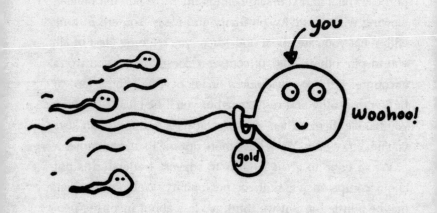

Chapter 12
BIG FOOT

· · · · · ·

You'll have been irked by the footballers' clichéd nonsense of giving 120 per cent. For years, I would hear that claptrap and scream at the TV, 'you cannot give more than 100 per cent, idiot'. To all the footballers ever, I apologize. If humble pie had calories, I'd be the fattest man in the world.

From footballers to southern African 'ubuntu' and then on to anteaters, Taoism and morphogenesis, this is indeed a chapter that takes eclectic to new heights.

We explain why everything's going to be a bit muffled at your funeral and then stay with a religious metaphor before leading into our grand finale – terror. Just in case we haven't inspired you, we're going to scare the living shit out of you.

In the unlikely event of sweet dreams, we'd like to thank you for having us. If you lie awake tonight, cursing us, we'd *still* like to thank you for having us.

To continue the footballing clichés, we're over the moon that you've got this far.

Sick as a Parrot

A prayer for modern times ...

Dear God

So far today I've done alright. I haven't gossiped. I haven't lost my temper. I haven't been greedy, moody, nasty or selfish. And I'm really glad about that. But in a few minutes, God, I'm going to get out of bed and from then on I'm going to need a lot more help. Thank you.

Amen

You've got this far, so we're going to credit you with good taste in leadership books, a certain degree of stickability and a wedge of intelligence. You've twigged that there have been two principal themes:

1. It's *not* about you. Your focus has to be on your people, *and* ...
2. It's *all* about you. If you're not inspired, your people don't stand a cat-in-hell's chance.

This headache of a contradiction is one or all of an oxymoron, juxtaposition and paradox. It brings us full circle, to the notion that your job as a leader is not to inspire people, but to be inspired. You have to give 120 per cent.

Yes we know! It used to irritate us too. *'Giving 120 per cent'* is one of those irritating football clichés up there with *'sick as a parrot'* and *'it's a game of two halves'*. For years, my personal bug-bear was *'giving 120 per cent'*. I'm an educated man so I'd curse at the radio, *'You cannot give more than 100 per cent!'*

But of course, the footballers are absolutely correct. You can give 120 per cent if the end result is that you have surprised yourself and achieved beyond what you thought was possible. This is why this book is so powerful, it's about enabling you to get your staff to go *beyond* what they thought they were capable of.

The only catch is that YOU have to go there first.

A massive part of your role is to create the environment where all your people flourish. Just imagine the creativity, motivation, banter, good will and energy if every single one of your team were turning up to work as the very best version of themselves.

We're rather taken with the Maori word *whakapapa*, a concept that implies a stewardship of the past, represented in rituals and responsibilities, but also a vested interest in creating a wonderful future. It rises way above shareholder value, corporate responsibilities and profit, tying in with another wonderful word, *ubuntu*: 'What you leave behind is not what is engraved in stone monuments, but what is woven into the lives of others.'

Jonas Salk translates it rather nicely as the belief that 'Our first responsibility is to be a good ancestor'. Gavin Oattes says it equally stunningly with his question, 'do you want to be the best *in* the world or the best *for* the world?' [85]

All along, we've been talking about *ubuntu*, so much so that we're tempted to finish the book, really abruptly, right now, with our version of *ubuntu* which says, *you've got 4000 weeks to make a dent in the universe. What are you doing about it?*

But there's a bit of the wider world of positive psychology that is missing. It's the spark plug bit – small but highly significant.

'Flourishing' is when an individual feels happy and this positivity is transmitted to their work colleagues. In such instances, the multiplier effect could be felt within the organization's suppliers, business partners, work colleagues and customers. But, of course, the leadership multiplier effect is so much bigger than that. Sandee Tisdale and Marcie Pitt-Catsouphes[86] found that a child's sense of well-being is affected less by the long working hours of their parents and more by their mood on returning home. Their conclusion is that working long hours in a job one loves is better for family relations than working shorter hours and coming home unhappy. That might trigger some bigger changes than anything else you've read!

You've invested a few quid in this book. If you implement the ideas, you should come home less exhausted and in a happier frame of mind than you used to, so your family feels the benefit. If your team are also feeling valued, listened to and, yes, loved, they will go home with a spring in their step too. So your positive influence reaches your family as well as having positive effects on your team's families ... this is getting to be seriously like *ubuntu*!

Stay Lucky

Fact: you are the person you've decided to be.

You have created you.

On reflection, a lot of the themes of this book fall into the category of the bleedin' obvious. But are they?

Consciousness involves the experience of knowing and the awareness of the known. Choice emerges from consciousness. If you are not conscious of something, you cannot choose it. Some stuff is only obvious once someone has pointed it out.

You're welcome.

'Terror Management Theory' posits that cultural worldviews including religious beliefs act as a 'shield designed to control the potential for terror that results from awareness of the horrifying possibility that we humans are merely transient animals groping to survive in a meaningless universe, destined only to die and decay'. Hardly a chucklefest.[87]

As we see it, while you're waiting to die and decay, you may as well keep busy. Groping for meaning doesn't mean you can't enjoy the ride. Sometimes (although not very often) life will go as planned and it'll be a doddle.

But mostly, life will be a white-knuckle hang-on-for-dear-life affair.

It's clichéd to talk about a roller-coaster of emotions but, actually, if you stick with it, it's quite a handy analogy. It's hard to enjoy the gentle *click click click* as you get higher because you know there's likely to be a sheer drop any time soon. We want you to learn to enjoy the *click click clicking* AND, here's the tricky bit, the swooshing, twisting and sometimes stomach-churning upside down bits too.

Applied to leadership and life, the downs are inevitable.

It's easy to snuggle underneath the duvet of excuses. Life's not fair, right? There really is too much work pressure, your boss really is a bit of a dick, work is imperfect, your commute is genuinely too long, the alarm does ring too loudly and too early, the weekends are short (actually, what is this five days on two days off thing? We reckon it's time for a rethink on that), the weather is truly grim, you cannot get a doctor's appointment, TV programmes really are abysmal, beer is too expensive, footballers really do earn too much, trains are irregular, getting your car serviced at a main dealer means you might have to sell a kidney ...

It's all true!

It's a massive advantage if you begin from a different starting point. Let's roll back the years to when your mum and dad met. At some point they will have started dating, kissing and fumbling awkwardly. I don't want to gross you out but in order for you to exist, your mum and dad must have had sex at least once. Hopefully, it was just a one-off, and you can now get the image out of your head. The gross bit is what your dad did – he exploded about 500 million sperm into your mum. Yes, of course it's horrific but hang in there, because in actual fact that was your first outing. You swam for dear life and out of 500 million, you were the tadpole that got to the egg first.

You are that sperm! *WooHoo!* You are already amazingly successful, the gold medallist sperm front crawler (possibly more of a wriggle? I don't know, I wasn't there).

But, hang on, you need to factor in the chances of your grandparents meeting and your grandad doing the same 500 million exploding sperm thing. Yes, with your grandma! Beyond horrific! And back through your lineage to whomever started the whole shebang. Depending on which belief system you adhere to, the chances are you'd have to trace it all the way back to Eve and Adam or us emerging gills flapping from the marshes. I think Ali Binazir's calculation of 1 in $10^{2,685,000}$ is more like it?[88]

Remember, you were the only successful sperm – there are 499,999,999 of your dad's tadpoles, shaking their little spermy fists, screaming that's its unfair that *they* didn't make it. So rather than grumbling that life's not fair, start from the realization that nobody actually ever said it was. That cuts out 95 per cent of your low-level grumbling.

......

WHEN HIS LIFE WAS RUINED, HIS FAMILY KILLED, HIS FARM DESTROYED, JOB KNELT DOWN ON THE GROUND AND YELLED UP TO THE HEAVENS, 'WHY GOD? WHY ME?' AND THE THUNDERING VOICE OF GOD ANSWERED, 'THERE'S JUST SOMETHING ABOUT YOU THAT PISSES ME OFF.'

......

Stephen King, **Storm of the Century** *(1999)*

There's a lot less huffing and puffing when you realize that leadership is supposed to be challenging. There's fewer histrionics when the penny drops that change is going to keep on coming whether you want it to or not. There's a much calmer response when you understand that sometimes wi-fi just won't be available. And yes, some customers will demand their money back.

Our advice? Chill. You were born lucky. You've cashed in at life's casino. Rejoice that, against all odds, you're here at all. Anything else is just a bonus.

Pronoia

Taoism has a word 'te' which refers to humans' moral action that is in accord with the way of their nature. Other books might call it authenticity? Alan Watts says, with te, 'one might become the kind of person who, without intending it, is a source of marvellous accidents'.[89]

When you think about the bosses or leaders you have had in the past, maybe one will stand out as being the *source of marvellous accidents* – the best boss you ever had, the one who grew you to 120 per cent, who you would do anything for. There's a big fat chance that if they died next week you'd go to their funeral.

So how do the great ones do it? How do they make you feel like that and get you to be so engaged? The discretionary effort you're prepared to give them is almost limitless and you just love them for it – but why? We think it's unlikely to be an accident.

Everyone knows about paranoia – the bastards are out to get you. But few are conversant with the opposite, *pronoia*, that sneaky suspicion that people are saying nice things behind your back.

Hence wouldn't this be a fabulous future scenario. After you've read this book, you pass it on to a colleague who reads it and also passes it on. You go about your working life, implementing our simple ideas and creating flourishing teams when, two years later, the book turns up in your office. *I remember that book*, you think fondly. *It was the one where they tried to suggest Bob the Builder was an inspirational leader. #Lol.* You pick it up, smiling. The book is battered, bruised and well-thumbed. You leaf through a few pages. Some corners are turned and some of your colleagues have scribbled notes in the margins.

One of the turned corners is page 137, the activity where they listed their best boss ever. And it was you. Yes, the bastards have been saying lovely things about you behind your back.

So our final top tip: *be the leader you wish you had.*

Dr Hindsight

Here's a quick aside from back in the day – I won't bore you with the minutiae, suffice to say it was a Sunday afternoon and I was busy preparing a presentation for the next day. It was going to be the full-on PowerPoint experience. It was the early days of PowerPoint and I'd just been on a one-day workshop that had taught me how to make points fly in. So, there I was, refining my slides so that every single point flew in. Some came from the side. Some swished from the top. I think some of them made 'swoosh' noises?

And then I found a special effect that revealed the letters one at a time. 'OMG!' hadn't been invented which is a shame as it would have fitted perfectly.

Ollie's footsteps tramped up the stairs. He was three and a bit. *'Daddy,'* he puffed, *'do you want to come and have a kick-about in the garden?'*

I didn't actually take my eyes off the screen. I was just about to preview a slide that would miraculously dim all the other points on the slide, except the one you were talking about. It was magic. Almost witchcraft!

Chapter 12 Big Foot

'In a bit fella. I'm in the middle of something.'

'When's in a "bit"?' he asked earnestly.

'Five minutes,' I promised, shooing him away with my hand. *'Just gimme five minutes to get this right.'*

And, bless him, off he went, good as gold. Except he didn't go very far. He plonked himself just outside the door and started counting, aloud. He was basically counting to 60, five times. First time around he got stuck on the transition between 49 and 50. He missed the 50s out and went straight to 60. And, if I'm being honest, that bugged me a bit because that gave me 10 seconds less.

He proudly got to 60 for the fifth time and announced in a hide and seek *'coming ready or not'* kind of chirpy voice that my five minutes were up.

'Are they indeed,' I snapped as he bounded back into the back bedroom cum office. *'First of all, your counting was all skew-whiff. And secondly, how on earth was I expected to concentrate with you out there, putting me off?'*

My three-year-old looked a little crestfallen. After all, I had promised. And all he wanted was a kick-about with his dad. But I was on a roll. *'And anyway,'* I snapped, *'I meant a looong five minutes, not a short five minutes.'*

His crestfallen face had now become confused, which I thought was good. Tie him up in knots and he'll leave me alone. *'So you go downstairs, get your trainers on and start the kick-about without me. And when I've finished this, I'll come out and play.'*

'Promise?'

'*Promise,*' I lied.

He tramped downstairs and got his shoes on. I heard him ask his mum, '*Is there such thing as a loooong five minutes?*' before I glanced outside and, there he was, banging the ball against the garage door. Phew! And I got on with adjusting my slides to the point that they were perfect. Perfect, that is, so long as my aim was to bamboozle the audience and completely detract from what I was actually saying.

Two hours later, I was finished!

I went downstairs and Ollie was asleep on the sofa, a *Bob the Builder* DVD cheerily lighting up the lounge. He'd worn himself out playing football on his own.

Now I could tell you that's not a big deal. Or that it doesn't matter. I could make a compelling case that I was genuinely busy, trying to prepare for work. And I could lie to you and say that work was very important and I was right to prioritize things in the way I did.

But, you see, it is a big deal. Because that's just one example. And there are a million others where I've got my priorities wrong.

We've been hoodwinking you all the way. This book isn't really about work. It's much bigger than that.

How we spend our days is, of course, how we spend our lives. Life is the culmination of the little things and it's these little things that make the big thing that is your life. Taking the principles of relationships, listening, empathy, being present, encouraging – and applying them at *home* – that's a game changer.

God and The Terminator

Being religious is associated with elevated happiness. The suggestion is that religion provides a framework of meaning as well as a collective identity and a reliable social network for people with like-minded views and values. Thus, ultimately, it is the strong social connections that provide happiness in a religious context. The result is the rather powerful effect whereby individuals give up their weekends to attend their place of worship and actually pay to do it!

It may be that the challenge for organizational designers is to create a similar cohesiveness, akin to a 'spiritual home' where, instead of religion, employees are bonded by a common purpose and/or pervading sense of 'why?' The organization creates a sense of community where high quality connections are the norm and where individual employees are playing to their strengths. In short, the challenge is to create a culture in which employees want to be part of something worthwhile and where engagement is not forced but, rather, it flows. Continuing the religious metaphor it, may be that this sense of higher purpose and internal buy-in is, indeed, a more enlightened way to create flourishing organizations.

This is all interesting, if a little overly philosophical.

Throughout this book we've been doing our level best to convince, persuade, cajole and inspire you. There is just one tactic left – terror – which we've divided into two parts, 'future near' and 'future far'.

It's easy to miss the obvious and to career through your career in a frenzy of busyness only to get to the other end and reflect with a PhD in Hindsight. It'll look so obvious from the future! So let's go there.

In 'future near' (but hopefully not-too-near), we'd like to have a final word on your 4000 weeks. When your time is up, we don't think it's death that scares most people, more the thought that they've not quite lived the go-getting ebullient life they might have hoped for.

After your time has passed, fingers crossed there'll be a bit of a do where a whole load of relatives, friends and hangers-on will gather. Some will be there purely for the vol-au-vents, but most will be there because they knew you. We don't want you to get paranoid, but you will be their sole focus of their conversations. Yes, the whole gig will revolve around stories of you! Very few of the conversations will be about what was on your 'to-do list' and almost all the chatter will be about who you were being while you were going about your 4000 weeks.

We're rather hoping that some former work colleagues might turn up. That's always a sign that you got your leadership approach more or less right. It might be nice to spend a couple of minutes imagining you're there, ear-wigging on their future conversations. Yes, it'll sound a bit muffled from inside your box, but we're really hoping that you will have adopted the advice in this book, in which case, you'll need a lot of sandwiches to feed a lot of people and the bar will run dry. There will be sadness for sure, but a whole load of grinning too.

Chapter 12 Big Foot

And the *final* final word of terror is about 'future far'. The first *Terminator* movie was Schwarzenegger's breakthrough movie, a low budget classic that stands the test of time. Copyright laws mean that I'm not allowed to quote the exact dialogue so let me describe a particularly tense scene. Arnie is a Terminator, a killing machine, sent from the future, whose aim is to track down a lady called Sarah Conner and eliminate her. He's dressed in leathers, with cool shades, has a sawn-off shotgun tucked into his belt and is riding a Harley. You really wouldn't want to mess with him. And a good guy is also tracking Sarah Conner, his mission being to save her from Arnie.

With me? Anyway, there's a very tense scene where the good guy has got Sarah Conner in a car, he grabs the scruff of her neck and tries to explain about the Terminator. He says something along the lines of, *'Listen and understand. It's out there, looking for you. It doesn't feel pity or remorse or fear and it absolutely will not stop, ever.'*

And I think you can substitute 'change' into that dialogue and it still makes sense. *'Listen and understand. CHANGE is out there, looking for you. It doesn't feel pity or remorse or fear and it absolutely will not stop, ever, until you are dead.'*

Remember page one, about the inevitability of change. Our ridiculous but true prediction of Apple going belly up? We're hoping change isn't quite as scary as the Terminator coming at you with a shotgun, but I guarantee it's going to keep coming, shapeshifting as a new competitor, technology, legislation, restructure, rising customer expectations or all of the above. This requires you to shake yourself out of thinking that change is a '6-month thing' to get through and then we can get back to normal. We're not saying change is necessarily good. Our argument is that by seeing it as inevitable, normal even, makes it a whole lot easier to deal with.

The very best way to be change-proof is to be positive about yourself and continually invest in your skills, knowledge and attitude. Reading this book and applying the principles will not only inoculate you from the 'change bug', it will also protect those around you. Better still, the leadership multiplier effect means that your positivity is not just a ripple. Get it right and you create a tsunami of engagement that sweeps through your work colleagues, their families and their communities. Don't forget to factor in the ripple at home too.

Life is happening and it's happening fast. You only get to live life once and you only get to experience each moment once. The stakes couldn't be higher.

Terror-wise, you can panic and look at how many precious weeks you've frittered away, acting out being ordinary. Inspiration-wise, you can look at what you have left and take action, be inspired and go beyond what you thought you were capable of. The terrifying brevity of life can act as an impetus to change. If you want to make a dent in the universe then that change doesn't start next week, next month, or with someone else.

If you've got this far you'll have realized when and with whom.

Hasta la vista, baby.

••••••

YOUR AUTHOR TAG TEAM

Mike Martin is an IT geek, turned good guy. He's got oodles of experience in the real world, delivering large change projects and, for the most part, retaining his zest and sense of humour along the way. Mike's Welsh, which helps.

He also delivers our flagship workshop 'The Art of Being Brilliant' in businesses and schools. His mission is to make Wales even more brilliant.

mike@artofbrilliance.co.uk

@mikemartinaob

Jonathan Peach (JP) has a background in retail management. He then went and did something completely stupid – jacking in a perfectly good career and retraining as a trainer and coach. As a result, JP woke up. His mission is now to help others open their eyes to the magnificence of life.

JP delivers 'The Art of Being Brilliant' as well as a host of other workshops on purpose, strengths and leadership.

jon@artofbrilliance.co.uk

@gobebrilliant

Andy Cope is an author and learning junkie who has recently qualified as the UK's first ever 'Dr of Happiness'. Yes, he knows it's a terrible title but it gives him a media platform that he's determined to milk for all it's worth. Andy believes there's never been a better time to refocus from human misery to human flourishing.

Andy is a sought-after keynote speaker who is lucky enough to work with businesses and school across the world.

andy@artofbrilliance.co.uk

@beingbrilliant

NOTES

Chapter 1

1 Adams, D. (1979). *The Hitchhiker's Guide to the Galaxy*. London: Pan Books.

2 Deresiewicz, W. (2014). *Excellent Sheep: The Miseducation of the American Elite and the Way to a Meaningful Life*. Simon & Schuster Children's Publishing.

3 Radcliffe, S. (2012). *Leadership: Plain and Simple*. 2nd Ed. London: Financial Times Series.

4 Laloux, F. and Wilber, K. (2014). *Reinventing Organizations: A Guide to Creating Organizations Inspired by the Next Stage of Human Consciousness*. Nelson Parker

5 Stairs, M. and Gilpin, M., (2010). 'Positive engagement: from employee engagement to workplace happiness'. In: Linley, P. A., Harrington, S. and Garcea, N. eds, *Oxford Handbook Of Positive Psychology And Work*. Oxford University Press.

6 Bolchover, D. (2005). *The Living Dead: Switched Off, Zoned Out - The Shocking Truth About Office Life*. Capstone.

7 Silver, K. (2017). 'Third of mothers' experience mental health issues'. [online] BBC News. Available at: http://www.bbc.co.uk/news/health-42140028; Muckett, J (2018). 'Third of accountants suffer from poor mental health'. [online] *Economia*. https://economia.icaew.com/en/news/january-2018/third-of-accountants-suffer-from-poor-mental-health; Bulman, M. (2017).

Notes

'Third of young people say their mental health has deteriorated since Brexit vote, survey shows'. [online] *Independent*. http://www.independent.co.uk/news/uk/home-news/young-people-mental-health-brexit-vote-financial-worries-income-rent-costs-eu-leave-a7972556.html

8   Marsh, N. (2008). 'How to make work-life balance work'. [video] Available at: https://www.ted.com/talks/nigel_marsh_how_to_make_work_life_balance_work

9   Hare, D. (2016). *The Buddha in me, the Buddha in you. A Handbook for Happiness*. Rider.

Chapter 2

10 Erhard, W., Jensen, M.C. and Zaffron, S. (2007). *Integrity: Where Leadership Begins: A New Model of Integrity.* Harvard Working Paper No. 07-03. [pdf] Available at: SSRN: https://ssrn.com/abstract=983401 or http://dx.doi.org/10.2139/ssrn.983401

11 George, J. M. (1990). 'Personality, affect, and behaviour in groups'. *Journal of Applied Psychology*, 75, pp. 107-116.

12 Christakis, N. and Fowler, J. (2011). *Connected: The Amazing Power of Social Networks & how they Shape our Lives.* Harper Press.

13 Achor, S. (2011). *The Happiness Advantage: The Seven Principles that Fuel Success & Performance at Work.* Virgin Books.

14 George, J. M. and Bettenhausen, K. (1990). 'Understanding pro-social behaviour, sales performance, and turnover: a group-level analysis in a service context'. *Journal of Applied Psychology*, 75, pp. 698–709.

15 Cameron, K. (2008). *Positive Leadership; Strategies for Extraordinary Performance.* Berrett-Koehler.

16 Gaffney, M. (2011). *Flourishing: How to Achieve a Deeper Sense of Well-being, Meaning & Purpose – Even When Faced with Adversity.* Penguin.

17 Pescosolido, A.T. (2001). *Emotional Intensity in Groups.* Unpublished doctoral dissertation, Case Western Reserve University, Cleveland, Ohio.

Chapter 3

18 Løgstrup, K.E. (1997). *The Ethical Demand*. University of Notre Dame Press.

19 Radcliffe, S. (2012). *Leadership: Plain and Simple*. 2nd ed. Financial Times Series.

20 Laloux, F. and Wilber, K. (2014). *Reinventing Organizations: A Guide to Creating Organizations Inspired by the Next Stage of Human Consciousness*. Nelson Parker

Chapter 4

21 Sirota, D., Mischkind, L.A. and Meltzer, M.I. (2005). *The Enthusiastic Employee*. Wharton School Publishing.

22 Rath, T. (2007). *Strengths Finder 2.0: A New & Upgraded Edition of the Online Test from Gallup's Now Discover Your Strengths*. Gallup Press.

23 Gallup.com, (2018). 'Gallup Q EMPLOYEE ENGAGE-MENT Survey'. [online] Available at: https://q12.gallup.com/public/en-us/Features

24 Dutton, J. E. (2014). *Build High Quality Connections in How to be a Positive Leader: Insights from Leading Thinkers on Positive Organizations*. Dutton, J. E. and Spreitzer, G. M. (Eds.). Berrett-Koehler.

25 Fredrickson, B. (2009). *Positivity: Ground-Breaking Research to Release your Inner Optimism & Thrive*. Oneworld.

26 Robinson, K. and Aronica, L. (2009). *The Element: How Finding Your Passion Changes Everything*. Penguin Books.

27 Spreitzer, G. M. and Porath, C. (2014). *Enable Thriving at Work in How to be a Positive Leader: Insights from Leading Thinkers on Positive Organizations. Small Actions Big Impact*. Dutton, J. E. and Spreitzer, M. (Eds.). Berrett-Koehler.

28 Bakker, A. B. and Demerouti, E. (2008). 'Towards a model of work engagement'. *Career Development International*, 13, pp. 209-223.

29 Bakker, A. B. (2009). *Building Engagement in the Workplace in The Peak Performing Organization*. Burke, R. J. & Cooper, C. L. (Eds.). Routledge, pp. 50–72

30 Baker, W., Cross, R. and Wooten, L. (2003). *Positive Organizational Network Analysis & Energizing Relationships in Positive Organizational Scholarship: Foundations of New Discipline*, pp 328-342. Cameron, K.S., Dutton, J.E. and Quinn, R.E. (Eds.). Berrett-Koehler.

31 Sinek, S (2016). *Together is Better: A Little Book of Inspiration*. Portfolio Penguin.

32 Gavin, J. H. and Mason, R. O. (2004). 'The virtuous organization: the value of happiness in the workplace'. *Organizational Dynamics*, 33(4), pp. 379-392.

33 Marsh, N. (2008). 'How to make work-life balance work'. [video] Available at: https://www.ted.com/talks/nigel_marsh_how_to_make_work_life_balance_work

34 Cameron, K. (2013). *Practicing Positive Leadership: Tools & Techniques that Create Extraordinary Results*. Berrett-Koehler.

35 Cameron, K. (2013). *Practicing Positive Leadership: Tools & Techniques that Create Extraordinary Results*. Berrett-Koehler.

36 Ipsos MORI Reputation Centre, (2011). 'FTSE 100 public reporting on employee wellness & engagement'. [pdf] Available at: https://www.ipsos.com/sites/default/files/publication/1970-01/Reputation_BITC_FTSE_100_Research.pdf

Notes

Chapter 5

37 A summary of the t-test results show p-values <.05 in 15 of the 16 affects measured. In order to limit the probability of type- 1 errors, the Bonferroni correction was used, adjusted the p-value to a more stringent 0.003. Post hoc comparisons using t-test with Bonferroni correction revealed significant results (p <.003) for the following workplace affects: enthusiasm, joy, inspiration, excitement, nervousness, anxiety, tension, worry, calmness, depression, dejection, despondency and hopelessness. The data for 'laid back' indicated a non-significant result (t(193) = .684, p = .475). Applying the Bonferroni correction, 'relaxed' (t(193) = 2.55, p = .012) and 'at ease' (t(193) = 2.74, p = .007) also reveal non-significant results.

Chapter 6

38 Taylor, S. E. and Brown, J. D. (1988). 'Illusion and well-being: a social psychological perspective on mental health'. *Psychological Bulletin*, 103, pp. 193-210.

39 Losada, M. and Heaphy, E. (2004). 'The role of positivity and connectivity in the performance of business teams: a nonlinear dynamics model'. *American Behavioural Scientist*, 47, pp. 740–65.

40 Gottman, J. (1994). *What Predicts Divorce? The Relationship between Marital Processes & Marital Outcomes*. Erlbaum Hillsdale: NJ.

41 Carnegie, D. (2006). *How to Win Friends and Influence People*. Vermilion.

42 Stanier, M.B. (2016). *The Coaching Habit: Say Less, Ask More & Change the Way You Lead Forever*. Box of Crayons Press.

Notes

Chapter 7

43 Hobbes, T. (2017). *Leviathan*. CreateSpace Independent Publishing Platform.

44 Michaels, E. and Handfield-Jones, H. (2001). *The War for Talent*. Harvard Business Review Press.

45 Ferris, T. (2007) *The 4-hour Workweek*, Crown Publishers, 2007.

46 Whitmore, J. (2002). *Coaching For Performance: Growing People, Performance and Purpose*. 3rd ed. Nicholas Brealey Publishing.

47 Stanier, M.B. (2016). *The Coaching Habit: Say Less, Ask More & Change the Way You Lead Forever*. Box of Crayons Press.

48 Goleman, D. (2000). 'Leadership that gets results'. *Harvard Business Review*.

49 Maslow, A.H. (2013). *A Theory of Human Motivation*. Wilder Publications.

50 Gordon, E., Barnett, K.J., Cooper, N.J., Tran, N. and Williams, L.M. (2008). 'An "integrative neuroscience" platform: application to profiles of negativity and positivity bias'. *Journal of Integrative Neuroscience*, 7(03), pp. 345-366.

51 Fredrickson, B. L. (2001). 'The role of positive emotions in positive psychology: the broaden-&-build theory of positive emotions'. *American Psychologist*, 56, pp. 218–226.

52 Aigner, G. (2011). *Leadership Beyond Good Intentions: What it takes to really make a difference*. Allen and Unwin.

53 Fredrickson, B. L. (2013). 'Positive Emotions Broaden and Build' in *Advances in Experimental Social Psychology* 47, pp. 1–54. Devine, P. & Plant, A. (Eds.). San Diego, CA: Academic Press.

54 McGregor, D.M. (1957). Adventure in thought and action. *Fifth Anniversary Convocation of the School of Industrial Management*.

Chapter 8

55 Kerr, J. (2013). *Legacy*. Constable.

56 Cameron, K.S. and Winn, B.(2011). 'Virtuousness in organizations'. In: G.M. Spreitzer and K.S Cameron eds., *The Oxford Handbook of Positive Organizational Scholarship*. Oxford University Press.

57 Spreitzer, G.M., and Sonenshein, S. (2003). 'Positive deviance and extraordinary organizing'. In: K. Cameron, J. Dutton, and R. Quinn eds., *Positive Organizational Scholarship: Foundations of a New Discipline*. Berrett-Kohler, pp. 207-224.

58 Cooperrider, D. and Whitney, D. (2005). *Appreciative Inquiry: A Positive Revolution in Change*. Berrett-Koehler.

59 Adapted from Cameron, K. (2008). *Positive Leadership; Strategies for Extraordinary Performance*. Berrett-Koehler, p. 8

60 Quoted in Cameron, K.S., Dutton, J.E., and Quinn, R.E. (2003). *Positive Organizational Scholarship*. Berrett-Koehler, pp.48-65.

61 Diener, E., Lucas, R.E. and Scollon, C. N. (2006). 'Beyond the hedonic treadmill: revising the adaptation theory of wellbeing'. *American Psychologist*, 61, pp. 305–314.

62 Siegel, D.J. (2010). *Mindsight: The New Science of Personal Transformation*. Bantam Books.

63 Pontefract, D. (2017). 'If culture comes first, performance will follow'. [online] Forbes. Available at: https://www.forbes.com/sites/danpontefract/2017/05/25/if-culture-comes-first-performance-will-follow/#76fa1a956e62

64 McDermott, S. (2007). *How to be a Complete and Utter Failure in Life, Work and Everything: 44 1/2 steps to lasting underachievement*. Pearson.

65 Achor, S. (2013). *Before Happiness: Five Actionable Strategies to Create a Positive Path to Success*. Virgin Books.

Notes

Chapter 9

66 Zander, R.S. and Zander, B. (2006). *The Art of Possibility: Transforming Professional and Personal Life*. Penguin.

67 *Time*, (1999). 'Person of the Century'. *Time*, 154(27).

68 *Time*, (1999). 'Person of the Century'. *Time*, 154(27).

69 Clifton, D.O. and Harter, J.K. (2003). 'Investing in strengths'. In: K.S. Cameron, B.J.E. Dutton & C.R.E. Quinn eds. *Positive Organizational Scholarship*. Berrett-Koehler Publishers, pp. 111-121.

70 Buckingham, M. and Clifton, D.O. (2005). *Now, Discover Your Strengths: How to Develop Your Talents & Those of the People You Manage*. Pocket Books.

71 Buckingham, M. and Clifton, D.O. (2005). *Now, Discover Your Strengths: How to Develop Your Talents & Those of the People You Manage*. Pocket Books.

Chapter 10

72 Cameron, K. (2013). *Practicing Positive Leadership: Tools & Techniques that Create Extraordinary Results*. Berrett-Koehler.

73 Cameron, K. and Levine, M. (2006). *Making the Impossible Possible*. Berrett-Koehler.

74 Baumeister, R.F. and Vohs, K. D. (2002). 'The pursuit of meaningfulness in life'. In: C.R Snyder and S.J Lopez eds. *The Handbook of Positive Psychology*. Oxford University Press, pp. 608-628.

Chapter 11

75 O'Reilly, C.A. and Chatman, J.A. (1996). 'Culture as social control: corporations, culture and commitment'. *Research in Organizational Behaviour*, 18, pp. 157-200.

76 O'Reilly, C.A. and Chatman, J.A. (1996). 'Culture as social control: corporations, culture and commitment'. *Research in Organizational Behaviour*, 18, pp. 157–200.

77 Buchanan, L, (2010). 'Meet the Millenials'. *Inc.*, 32(7), p. 166.

78 Dahlgreen, W. (2015). '37% of British workers think their jobs are meaningless'. [online] YouGov. Available at: https://yougov.co.uk/news/2015/08/12/british-jobs-meaningless/

79 Hackman, J. R. and Oldham, G. R. (1975). 'Development of the Job Diagnostic Survey'. *Journal of Applied Psychology*, 60, pp. 159-170.

80 Hackman, J. and Oldman, G. (1976).' Motivation through the Design of Work: Test of a Theory'. *Organizational Behaviour & Human Performance*, 16, pp. 250-279.

81 Grant, A. M. (2014). 'Outsource Inspiration'. In: J.E. Dutton and G. Spreitzer eds, *How to be a Positive Leader: Small Actions Big Impact*. Berrett-Koehler.

82 Sinek, S. (2011). *Start with Why: How Great Leaders Inspire Everyone to Take Action*. Penguin.

83 Kahneman, D. (2012). *Thinking, Fast and Slow*. Penguin.

84 Zander, R.S. and Zander, B. (2006). *The Art of Possibility: Transforming Professional and Personal Life*. Penguin.

Notes

Chapter 12

85 Cope, A. and Oattes, G. (2018). *Shine: Rediscovering Your Energy, Happiness and Purpose*. Hodder.

86 Tisdale, S. and Pitt-Catsouphes, M. (2012). 'Linking social environments with the well-being of adolescents in dual-earner and single working parent families'. *Youth & Society*, 44, pp. 118–140.

87 Greenberg, J., Pyszczynski, T. and Solomon, S. (1986). 'The causes and consequences of a need for self-esteem: A terror management theory'. In: R.F. Baumeister ed., *Public Self and Private Self*. Springer-Verlag, pp.189-212

88 Binazir, A (2011). 'What are the chances of your coming into being?'. [Blog] Harvard Blog. Available at: http://blogs.harvard.edu/abinazir/2011/06/15/what-are-chances-you-would-be-born/

89 Watts, A. (1975). *The Way of Zen*. Thames & Hudson.